COMMUNICATING IN ORGANIZATIONS

Edward H. Rockey

UNIVERSITY
PRESS OF
AMERICA

LANHAM • NEW YORK • LONDON

Copyright © 1984 by

University Press of America,™ Inc.

4720 Boston Way
Lanham, MD 20706

3 Henrietta Street
London WC2E 8LU England

Printed in the United States of America

© copyright 1977 by Winthrop Publishers, Inc.

Photographs by Kim May.

Library of Congress Cataloging in Publication Data

Rockey, Edward H., 1928-
Communicating in organizations.

Reprint. Originally published: Cambridge, Mass. :
Winthrop Publishers, 1977.
1. Communication in management.   2. Communication in
organizations. I. Title.
[HF5718.R6   1984]   658.4'5   84-17232
ISBN 0-8191-3751-0 (pbk. : alk. paper)

All University Press of America books are produced on acid-free
paper which exceeds the minimum standards set by the
National Historical Publications and Records Commission.

To Ruth,
the best communicator
in our family organization

contents

three

Management Style and Communication 63

four

Planning For Communication 91

Contents

five

introduction

Think of an organization as a living body. The parts of the body represent various organizational functions. For example, the brain represents planning, and the skeleton represents the structure of the organization. If we continue this comparison, which part of the body will best represent communication?

Since communication pervades the entire organization, connecting and influencing all of its parts, no single part can represent communication accurately; however, the *nervous system* can represent communication. The nervous system carries impulses throughout the organism, coordinating the entire body. Therefore, we will understand the nature and function of communication more accurately if we think of communication as a system, connecting every element in the organization, than if we think of communication as one specific element.

A healthy organization requires effective communication. Poor communication lowers morale and reduces productivity. Some managers believe that poor communication wastes more time and money then any other organizational problem. Since communication has such a vital influence on the success of any organization, each individual in the organization should strive to communicate effectively and to continually improve as a communicator.

Probably because of the relationship between organizational success and effective communication, there is a relationship between communication skills and promotability. For example, subscribers to the *Harvard Business Review* rated the ability to communicate as the most important requirement for a promotable executive.[1]

Ordinarily there is also a relationship between job responsibility and the amount of time and skill devoted to communication activities: as responsibilities increase, more and more time and ability are required for communication. You can easily think of unskilled jobs where communication skills play a minor role. On the other hand, picture the communication involvement of managers.

Managers spend virtually their entire time at work in communication activities—interviewing and being interviewed, reading or dictating correspondence, assigning or studying reports, giving speeches to internal and external groups, discussing issues and decisions in committees and conferences. Other qualities being equal, employees who demonstrate an ability to communicate effectively will find themselves more promotable than those who communicate ineffectively.

Since communication plays such a vital role in organizational and personal success, you would expect that groups and individuals would (1) establish communication goals, (2) set and enforce useful communication policies, and (3) carry out procedures to fulfill such goals and policies. For example, an organization could set a goal committing the organization to improve morale by communicating with employees in a more timely and tactful way. Policies could then be established to help reach this goal. One such policy might require that employees learn about certain vital matters (big contracts, new products or services, expansion of the organization, important personnel changes) directly from the organization and not through outside sources such as newspapers, radio, or legislators. Then specific procedures could be worked out to control the timing and transmission of such information through the organization's media.

[1] Garda W. Bowman "What Helps or Harms Promotability?" *Harvard Business Review*, Jan.–Feb. 1964, p. 14.

Unfortunately, we do not always find such goals, policies and procedures in effect. Perhaps that is why the following irony exists: most managers consider themselves good communicators, yet one of the most frequently-heard gripes in many organizations is "Communication around here is rotten."

Whatever the status of communication in your organization, you can develop communication goals for yourself, and you can use your role to improve organizational communication. You can set goals to:

1. Transmit information accurately.
2. Listen attentively.
3. Use the most appropriate medium for a message.
4. Encourage feedback.
5. Organize messages meaningfully.
6. Employ a concise, clear style.
7. Adapt to audience needs and backgrounds.
8. Perceive nonverbal cues alertly.
9. Participate effectively in committees.
10. Conduct interviews successfully.
11. Write tactful letters.
12. Reduce communication barriers.
13. Give effective oral presentations.

The basic aim of this text is to help you fulfill such goals, so that you will be able to communicate more effectively in your organizational career.

one

Understanding How Communication Works

OBJECTIVES

After reading Chapter One you should understand how the following elements affect the communication process:

encoding
decoding
feedback
semantic confusion
nonverbal language
channels
barriers

In addition, after reading this chapter you should have gained insight into the influence which the following factors have upon the interpretation of messages:

cultural background
loyalties
expectations
education
concepts of the situation
values
personal interests
stereotypes

We take for granted some of the most complex life processes. Usually we don't even think about our most vital and fundamental activities, we simply do them. For example, at this very moment you are performing at least three complicated functions—circulating your blood, breathing, and reading. Even though we rarely analyze our capacity to carry out such activities, we depend upon them for survival. Without oxygen or circulated blood, we cannot live; without the ability to receive verbal messages, we cannot progress socially or economically.

As a first step toward developing our ability to communicate effectively, we must attempt to understand such intricate processes as speaking, reading, writing, and listening. Let me explain the words "must attempt." I say "must" because various studies have indicated that communication skills have a great deal to do with both promotability and successful social adjustment. I say "attempt" because of a frustrating reality—no one completely understands how communication takes place. But we don't completely understand most life processes, and still we continue to breathe, eat, sleep, dream, and fly to the moon. So I'll continue to write this book, and you'll continue to read it, I hope, because even if we can't understand communication completely, we can understand it helpfully and usefully.

SOME KEY ELEMENTS

One way to grasp the communication process involves building a model which includes the basic elements of communication. Typically, some individual or group wants to transmit a message to some other individual or group.

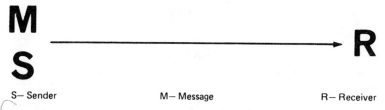

S— Sender   M— Message   R— Receiver

Unfortunately, most of us usually assume that "message sent is message received." This illusion has become a common barrier to effective communication; perhaps no greater barrier exists.

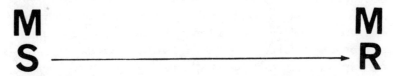

We tend to assume that if we send a memo with ideas or data the person receiving the memo will understand it just as we intended. But does this always occur? I received the following memo: "Please send me a photo and a brief biography. We need this very soon, as the printer is working on a deadline for the brochure." Probably the sender had a certain size and type of photo in mind, a particular length for the biography and a specific date for the printer's deadline; however, I did not know any of those details after reading the memo. In contrast to the "illusion of communication" model shown previously, the actual situation might be represented this way:

So I telephoned the sender, and he gave me sufficient additional information to enable me to comply with his instructions. We can call the telephone conversation a form of *feedback*, a term which we will define as the return of information so that error can be corrected and mutual understanding can be reached.

Feedback resembles an automatic thermostat system which controls heating and cooling. When the temperature of the room rises above or falls below a desired temperature, an electric signal goes out to the heater or the cooler. When the room reaches the desired temperature, another signal is

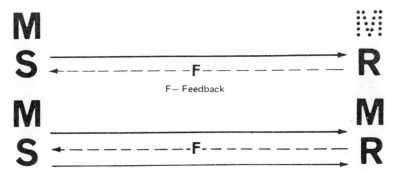

F— Feedback

sent, and the equipment is turned off. The directional device in a torpedo also serves as a feedback illustration: if the torpedo travels to the left or right of the target, the directional device puts it back on target.

As I type the manuscript for this book, my eyes become a source of feedback for my sense of touch. Occasionally, ("Blast it!") my eyes note that my fingers have not pressed the appropriate typewriter keys, and I go through a series of physical activities to correct the error.

Words . . . Words . . . Words

If a sender wants to transmit a message to a receiver or if the receiver wants to transmit feedback to the sender, some sort of symbols must be used, either verbal or nonverbal. We must now expand our model to include this concept, focusing for the moment on verbal forms (written or oral).

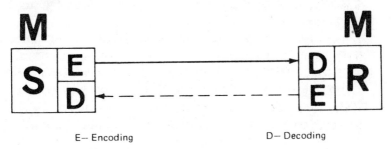

E— Encoding   D— Decoding

Encoding involves converting the message we have in our heads into symbols which can be transmitted. In the last chapter of this text we will consider specific spoken and written forms in organizational communication, but for now we will concentrate on the idea of a verbal symbol.

Try this experiment sometime: hold up your index finger and middle finger so that they form a "V"; then ask people what the symbol "means." Immediately you will probably get a number of conflicting answers—"peace," "rabbit ears," "two more please, waitress," "victory," and so on. Actually, the most productive response to your question would go something like this: "Well, that all depends upon what *you* mean by 'V.' Tell me what you 'mean,' and I'll tell you what 'V' 'means.' "

Obviously, "V" could have hundreds of meanings. Usually, when I do the experiment, I assume that "V" means Roman numeral five. Though I have conducted this little experiment with audiences totalling thousands of people, no one has ever guessed Roman numeral five. But just as "V" is an arbitrary symbol, with scores and scores of possible meanings, so every word in the dictionary is an arbitrary symbol. Essentially, *words don't mean; people mean.*

Going back to the confusing memo I received about the photo, what does "brief biography" mean? What does "very soon" mean? To one person "brief biography" could signify a fifty-word paragraph, while to another it would mean reducing a four-page biography to one page. Depending upon the individuals involved, "very soon" could mean two days or two weeks.

Obviously, the encoding-decoding process works more effectively when we use words that are less likely to be misunderstood, specifically avoiding vague terms. After telephoning the author of the memo, I discovered that what he "meant" was "please send me a 5″ × 7″ glossy portrait and a fifty- to sixty-word biography by noon on Friday, April 5."

If someone asked me what "round" meant, I would probably answer "circular" or "shaped like a ball or ring." What would you say? The dictionary on my desk has over seventy definitions for the word "round." In what sense is round one of a prize fight round? If you travel by plane with a round-trip ticket between Dallas and Chicago in what sense is your trip round? When a physician makes his or her rounds, must the doctor move in a circle? How can you round up cattle in a square barnyard? If it isn't round from January to December, how can you grow grass all year 'round? Perhaps by now your head is going 'round and 'round (even if it isn't moving in a circle).

Between the time a sender encodes a message, the symbols travel to the receiver, and the receiver decodes the symbols and translates them into a message, much can go wrong. When misunderstandings occur about the meaning of words, we call the problem *semantic confusion.*

Nonverbal Symbols

People in organizations send out virtually countless nonverbal messages every day. Perhaps this reality led to the expression, "You cannot not communicate." In other words, even if you decided not to speak all day or write anything, your *nonverbal language* would communicate constantly.

Your face talks through smiles and frowns. Your arms and hands punctuate. Your shoulders shrug. Your posture can sag or straighten up. Your walk can be brisk or laborious. Your handshake can be hearty or limp.

Do you stand close and "buttonhole" people or do you stand a couple of feet away? Do you keep a desk or other furniture between you and the other person? Is your office in or near the executive suite or is it far away from the center of power?

What quality stationery do you use? How distinctive is the artwork on your letterhead or calling card? Does your office have a window with a view? Do you arrive on time or early or late? Where do you sit at the conference table? What clothes are you wearing? Where and what do you eat for lunch?

Do you blush or hesitate? Did your inflection fall or rise when you said "I certainly will"? Did you pause and drop in volume when you replied, "Yes—I'd—be glad—to help—by staying late—tonight"?

Right or wrong, accurate or inaccurate, people tend to interpret the kinds of nonverbal cues given above. We find meanings in the use of time, distance and space, and people tend to decode nonverbal language as well as verbal language. Often we are more aware of the verbal cues we send out than we are of the nonverbal cues; we can plan verbal language carefully, but often we react nonverbally without being aware of or having control of our responses. At any rate, nonverbally, you cannot not communicate. You encode and decode nonverbal symbols every day.

Noise

The term noise applies to whatever interferes with the reception of information. We have all experienced electronic nosie when lightning caused static on the radio or when a shrill whistle came across a loudspeaker. Communication scholars have extended the concept of noise in a system to go beyond technical interference in mechanical systems and to include any kind of interference in interpersonal and organizational communication.

Of course, even physical noise can interfere in various organizational systems (loud machinery making discussion confusing or difficult, people talking nearby when you are making a telephone call); however, relationships, attitudes, feelings, and similar aspects seem more significant than mere physical noise. (The second half of this chapter will focus on these nonphysical aspects.)

But whether we're thinking of noise as the office grapevine or the loud jet passing overhead, we can represent this factor in our model in this way:

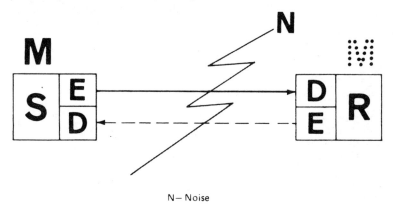

N— Noise

Much of the material in this text is devoted to reducing noise in organizational communication.

Channels

Encoded messages must pass through *channels* in order to reach a receiver. Such channels may range all the way from a simple memo format to a highly complex microwave system.

Some common media which serve as channels for vocal messages follow:

telephones	films
intercoms	television sets
loudspeakers	
radios	
tape recordings	

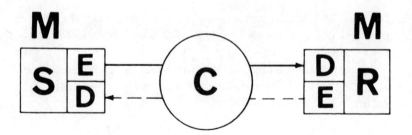

C— Channel(s)

Written channels include:

> letters
> memos
> bulletins
> books
> printed forms (e.g. invoices)
> minutes of meetings
> pamphlets
> handbooks and manuals
> magazines and newspapers

Often messages become distorted as they pass through channels. You may want to try the experiment in serial transmission suggested at the end of this chapter. By serial transmission we mean that a message goes through a number of transmissions (from person V to person W to person X to person Y to person Z and perhaps even back to person V, and so on). If you perform the serial transmission experiment, you will probably note most or all of the following occurring as information passes from V to W to X, and so on. A model of serial transmission would look like this:

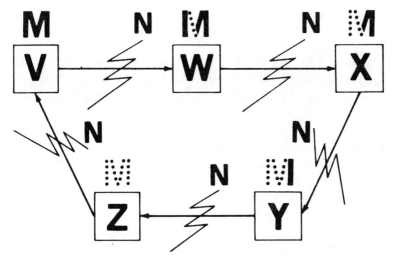

1. Details will be dropped.
2. Details will be added.
3. Details will be altered.
4. Inferences will become facts.
5. Personal interpretations will alter the tone and emphasis.

Probably the first example of serial distortion in organizations that we think of involves the rumor mill; however, messages become distorted in official, formal organizational channels as well. By the time messages travel from the executive suite, through management, and through supervision, the line employee may get a message quite different from the original. Often this situation can be improved by reducing the number of links in the communication chain (for example, having the head of the organization speak directly to employees through a public address system), using written messages, getting feedback, simplifying messages, and putting material in easy-to-read, orderly, and clear formats.

HOW PEOPLE INTERPRET MESSAGES

The new employee cafeteria has a mural painted on one wall. Two employees pass the mural for the first time. One thinks, "Well, they finally gave us something beautiful to look at around here," while the other murmurs, "They call that art? Garbage!"

One hundred police recruits view a training film, and then they fill out response forms, evaluating the film. On a five-point scale, some recruits judge the relevance of the film as poor, others as excellent. Some recruits describe the technical accuracy of the film as average, others as very poor.

An organization posts a bulletin on a board right next to the payroll window. The first employee to see it says, "Who cares?" The second moans, "Oh, no, not again!" A third exclaims, "Fantastic!"

At 3:30 P.M. a manager informs six subordinates that they must come to a brief meeting at 4:00 P.M. If we could read the minds of a few of the subordinates at 3:45, we might discover the following: "I hope we're not going to have any more layoffs." "I'll bet the work quota has been increased." "I wonder if the Director has resigned."

You could probably list dozens of similar examples. One that comes close to home for me involves faculty evaluation forms, in which students in the same class have rated me quite differently in response to identical questions. How can we account for such differences in interpretation?

General Cultural Background

Each of us has a cultural background—rural, urban or, suburban; lower, middle or, upper class, and so on. Out of such backgrounds we form habits of thought and patterns of judgment which influence our perception of meaning.

For example, many factory employees in Japan receive an understanding of life-long employment from their companies. But if an employee shows any interest in working for another company, the present employer will view the employee as extremely disloyal. In the United States, on the other hand, such loyalty rarely occurs. In fact, at the management level, executive search organizations (called "head hunters") make a living by enticing individuals to move from one company to another.

In Japan suicide has been viewed widely as an honorable way out, and Japan has one of the highest suicide rates in the world. But in some other cultures, suicide may be deemed "disgraceful" or "sinful."

In some nations public employees may go out on strike without risking punishment from the state. Thus, in many cities in the United States people working for police departments, fire departments, and other vital municipal services have gone out on strike. In certain other nations such action would be considered treasonable.

For our purposes, general cultural background includes such aspects as family, ethnic group, religion, education, nationality, and region of the country. We think, encode, transmit, and decode within the framework of such cultural factors, whether we are conscious of it or not. When backgrounds lack a common influence, people may have difficulty communicating.

Imagine a couple moving from one of the Southern states of the United States to a Northern city. During their entire lives they have heard store clerks say such things as: "How are you this evening?" ("Evening" in the Northeast means sunset to bedtime, and "evening" in the South means noon to sunset.) "May I help you?" "We appreciate your business," and "y'all come back and see us now, heah." Then this couple visit stores in their new neighborhood where some clerks come up and say, "Yes?" That's culture shock.

Other things being equal, the more we have in common
with another individual, the greater the likelihood that we
will be able to communicate effectively. As this cultural
overlap grows smaller, the likelihood that we will be able to
communicate effectively decreases. A cultural overlap, or
shared field of experience, may be represented this way:

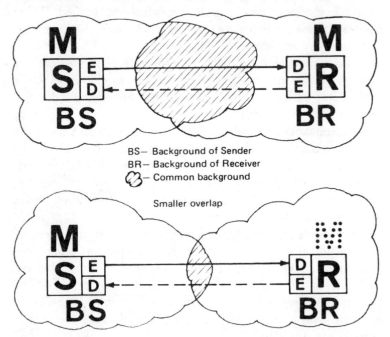

BS— Background of Sender
BR— Background of Receiver
— Common background

Smaller overlap

It is important to realize that not one person exists in
the entire world who has a background identical with yours
in every respect. Even the famous Siamese twins, Chang and
Eng, probably related to various individuals differently, experienced different stimuli, and so on, although they might
have approached identical fields of experience closer than
any other human beings. So, in each communication situation we must build on common experiences and allow for
the unique background of each individual involved.

Group Attachments

Growing out of our cultural backgrounds, we tend to identify with certain groups, to develop loyalties, and to accept norms. Often when we say "we" and "they" or "us" and "them" we imply group awareness and distinctness.

Most societies have *primary groups*, associations which involve personalized or intimate relationships. The family stands out as the most clear and powerful example, but we observe many others all around us—a long-standing car pool or coffee klatsch, a foursome who play golf, bridge, or tennis together weekly, a group of firefighters who work on the same shift, a hobby group, or a small synagogue. The values and attitudes of such groups tend to influence the way their members perceive messages.

We also tend to belong to less personal groups, such as political parties, professional associations, unions, and so on. Sometimes we belong to subgroups of these larger ones, such as the local support team for a political candidate or the local chapter of an occupational group. When our group officially endorses a particular idea or candidate, we tend to go along, to be loyal to the group.

When messages come to us which pertain to our group attachments, we will lean toward interpreting the messages in the light of our relationships. Generally speaking, we will tend to communicate more effectively with people who share our group loyalties and to have difficulty communicating with people who do not. The table on the following page shows stereotypes which I will use to illustrate this principle.

Let us assume that the machinist has sent a letter to the company magazine. The letter urges employees to write to their representatives regarding a bill before the legislature. The bill provides special educational benefits for the children of large low-income families, and funding will come from increased taxation of corporations and high personal

Person A	Person B
machinist, semi-skilled	executive
second generation American	sixth generation American
Eastern European parents	Anglo-Saxon ancestry
Roman Catholic	Presbyterian
Democratic Party	Republican Party
bowling club member	country club member
$4.89 per hour, wages	$55,000 per year, salary
six children	two children
high school diploma	college degree
union member	management club member

incomes. The letter has come to Person B, the executive, who must decide whether it should appear in the company paper, and, if so, whether a reply should accompany the letter in order to represent the opposing viewpoint. The executive's group loyalties influence the reaction to the letter.

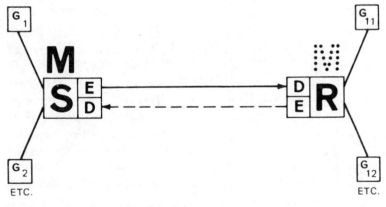

G — Group
G_1, G_2 — Groups to which Sender belongs
G_{11}, G_{12} — Groups to which Receiver belongs

Our Expectations

Imagine this experiment. Employees from a large corporation are randomly assigned to three groups, fifty in each group. Their task is to evaluate an organizational benefits handbook for possible use by the company. Before they fill out the questionnaire, two "experts" speak only to Group I, telling them that the handbook is obviously inferior and inaccurate; two "experts" speak only to Group II, assuring them that the handbook is obviously superior and accurate. Group III receives no orientation about the quality of the handbook. All three groups then have opportunity to look at the handbook and fill out the questionnaire. Based on earlier experiments, you would expect that Groups I and II would find what they expected to find and that Group II would give the handbook a higher rating than Group I. In effect, we "see" what we expect to see.

Education

Formal education can make a difference in communication, because our expertise with technical data, sophisticated processes, and complex ideas can help us in understanding and explaining. But informal education counts too. For example, no knowledgeable individual applying for a management job would ask, "What will the wages be?" For one thing, the term "wages" is never used to describe management compensation. In addition, the compensation package might include several types of benefits in addition to "salary," such as bonuses, stock options, deferred compensation, profit sharing, and so on. For some executives, such items may exceed the salary itself.

Sometimes we simply have to learn the jargon of the role or profession by listening, participating, and observing.

It's acceptable for a plumber to say, "I'm going to cut out that pipe and stick in a new one," but it's not acceptable for a surgeon to say, "I'm going to cut out your kidney and stick in a new one."

Concept of the Situation

When I was eighteen I walked into an Army barracks in Wisconsin and was greeted by these words, "Hey, Rockey, the Chaplain was looking for ya." Thinking it might be a joke, since, to my knowledge, the Chaplain had never come to our Battery looking for anyone, I checked with Battery Headquarters. He had been looking for me. I had never met the Chaplain. Why would he look for me? Chaplains often bear bad news, I thought. Terrifying scenes flashed through my mind: my parents had no doubt been in some disaster; my brother's ship must have gone down; perhaps my sister had some dread disease.

Unfortunately, it took quite a while to locate the Chaplain. He said something like this: "The chapel organist has been transferred, and I looked through the personnel files to see if I could find a Protestant who could play for us. I couldn't find anyone, but I noticed that you play the accordion. Would you be willing to play at our Sunday morning services?" I don't remember exactly what I said in reply, something about my amateurish ability and unwillingness to fulfill his request, but I do remember the great sense of relief when I learned why he wanted to see me.

If an employee comes in for a periodic review, and if that employee has come to perceive review situations as occasions when "you get chewed out," such a concept will influence the employee's interpretation of the review session. If we conceive of staff meetings as a "waste of time where nothing important ever happens," then we may interpret staff meetings in that light even if something productive does occur.

Value Systems

An individual's standards and ideals will strongly influence the interpretation of messages. Varying viewpoints of honesty and thrift cause us to interpret organizational policies and practices in different ways. A government employee recently discovered that the plane he planned to fly on was full, despite the fact that he had a ticket for that flight (the airline had overbooked that flight). A passenger agent told the government employee that a first-class seat could be arranged if the difference in fare were paid. The government employee refused the first-class space, explaining that flying first-class was "wasting the taxpayers' money." That flight crashed, killing all aboard. The ethics of individual employees rarely get newspaper space, unless they are dramatically involved, as in this case; nevertheless, millions of incidents every day reflect the varying ethical standards of employees.

Today many industries and citizens have considerable interest in ecological values. People interpret environmental issues differently, depending upon their interest in preserving fresh air, clean water, animal life, and the beauty of the landscape. Various viewpoints on the free enterprise system and what constitutes a reasonable profit influence the interpretation of ecological laws as well as of fair employment practices.

Personal Interest

Have you ever been aware that some people were talking nearby, without being aware of the actual words being spoken by these people, until your name was mentioned? Chances are that you then tuned in rather intensely.

Naturally we devote more intense attention to messages which seem to affect our destiny than to seemingly irrelevant messages. While reading a company newspaper, how much attention will employees give to reading a statement about company profits? "It all depends," you say? Right. It all depends upon such aspects as: Are the employees in a profit-sharing plan? Have possible layoffs been announced? Is some employee interested in seeing if some other employee has a boat advertised in the "Sell or Swap" section?

When we see a bulletin board, we tend to notice items which pertain to our personal welfare. In staff meetings we tend to interpret the validity of suggestions according to their probable effect upon our unit of the company or our personal goals.

Hardening of the Categories

This disease can really constrict the meaning of a message. Actually, in our more reasonable moments, we know that no two individuals, no two events, no two ideas, no two physical objects are exactly alike in every detail. But we use words to categorize people, happenings, concepts, and things. And categorize we must, because life would be too complex and bewildering if we made elaborate distinctions every time we discussed a topic. Imagine the absurdity, for example, of an employee typing a purchase order and including the words "although I fully realize that no two widgets are exactly alike in size or weight, please ship immediately ten gross of Model Q Widgets." If we have to pave a parking lot or build an airplane, we can't devote time to the startling and fascinating reality that no two pieces of gravel or no two rivets are exactly alike in every detail.

But stereotypes, too, can be absurd. Invented in the eighteenth century, the stereotype was a printing block which turned out copies which looked alike. Then the term was applied to the pictures in our heads which do not necessarily correspond to the reality of the data.

It matters little that no two sheets of paper are exactly alike, but it matters a great deal that no two accountants, no two Norwegians, no two union members, no two managers, no two women, no two police officers are alike. Yet we sometimes communicate, whether we're encoding or decoding, as if all members of a group were alike. Ethnically, take the Wukkas, for example: "When you've seen one Wukka, you've seen em all." Or take that famous political group, the Lukkas: "A Lukka is a Lukka is a Lukka." And then, occupationally, there are always the Tukkas: "That's a Tukka for you; they'll do it every time."

We know that no two salespeople or secretaries are exactly alike, no two blacks or whites, no two Republicans or Democrats, no two Italians or Germans. Very significant differences occur. In sending and receiving messages, our communication will reflect reality to the extent that we avoid hardening of the categories and make accurate, intelligent distinctions.

COMMUNICATION—A MODEL OF THE PROCESS

How can we be clear and comprehensive in summarizing the communication process in a single model? We can't. So many complexities apply to human communication that we must settle for something less than completeness and clarity. But we can summarize some of the most significant aspects of the process, and we can sharpen our awareness of what goes on when we attempt to send and receive messages.

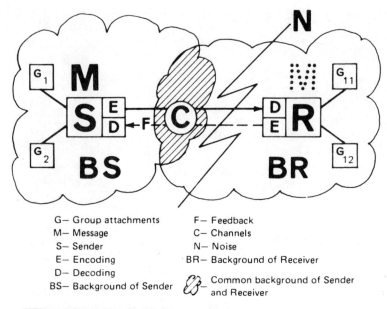

G— Group attachments   F— Feedback
M— Message   C— Channels
S— Sender   N— Noise
E— Encoding   BR— Background of Receiver
D— Decoding
BS— Background of Sender   Common background of Sender
                                 and Receiver

COMMUNICATION—A DEFINITION

Contemporary scholars have offered dozens of definitions
of communication, and it would be arrogant and unpro-
fessional to come up with "a definition to end all definitions"; however, I offer this working definition of effective
organizational communication:

> Effective organizational communication occurs when a
> sender transmits a message and a receiver responds to the
> message in a manner which satisfies the sender.

Note a few implications of this definition:

1. It focuses on *applied* communication. This brief text
deals with getting results through communicating effectively
in organizations; it does not deal with theories, experiments,
or philosophies which go beyond that goal. To think of an
analogy in the area of diet, it is more like a small book en-

titled, "How to Eat So You Stay Healthy" than a large volume entitled, "The Science of Nutrition."

2. It accepts the *satisfying* concept. In organizations, as in almost all human situations, we often accept what is less than perfect. As long as a situation becomes productive or meets our basic goals, we usually settle for it. Of course, this does not mean that leaders should not enforce some messages to the letter (for instance, requiring goggles at grinding machines), but it does mean that most of the time most of us live with a level of satisfaction which is less than ideal. Managers tend to settle for a productive understanding, rather than pressing for clarification of every historical, linguistic, philosophical, or technical aspect of a communication. The time and energy involved in reaching a "perfect" understanding (assuming for the moment that it is possible) would be too costly.

3. It assumes a *feedback loop*. In order to realize satisfaction, parties must get some sort of confirming response. This can be verbal or nonverbal, written or oral. It can occur through observation, suggestion systems, quality control reports, dialogue, sales, production, and so on, but somehow the sender must experience verification of an adequate understanding of the intent of the message. Of course, in the process of giving feedback, the receiver becomes a sender and the original sender becomes a receiver. In addition, the original sender may modify a message in the light of feedback. But at each stage, our definition assumes sufficient response to confirm adequate understanding.

CONCLUSION

When we pay attention to a stimulus, we tend to give it an interpretation, whether the stimulus is verbal or nonverbal.

We base our interpretations on such factors as our general backgrounds, our loyalties, our vocabularies, our education, our expectations, our personal interests, our values, and our prejudices. Because of such factors, distortions often occur as messages filter through channels. But by being aware of such factors, we can work toward encoding and decoding more effectively and toward reducing "noise" in organizational communication.

SKILL DEVELOPERS

1. List your own group attachments. How do these associations influence your communication behavior?
2. As you read each of the following terms, record the first word that pops into your head:

liberal	rich	male	poor
female	oriental	establishment	conservative
police	manager	black	union member
white	welfare	politician	youth

   Discuss your responses with someone else who has recorded theirs. What tendencies do you notice?
3. Pick up a book or magazine article or newspaper you have read recently.

Pretend that you are of a different:	For example, I, Ed Rockey, would have to become:
name	Suzanne Lavaud
sex	female
race	black
nationality	Haiti
educational background	eighth grade

occupation	sugar packaging
income	just above poverty level
religion	Roman Catholic
political viewpoint	nondemocratic
marital status	single

Look at the book or magazine article or newspaper again. What does it "mean" now?

4. You may want to attempt this serial transmission experiment in class. Ask four students to leave the room. Meanwhile, another student prepares notes in order to give a three-minute description of the classroom, including such features as size, decor, fixtures, flooring, color, lighting, heating or cooling system, furniture, windows, views, shape, and so on, including some personal opinions of taste or preference on several of these items. If we call the students V, W, X, Y, and Z, let's identify V as the one who prepared the description. W comes back in the room, and V gives the description to W, who must repeat it to X without notes, and so on until Z finally reports to V what Z has heard from Y. The rest of the class should record what happens to details and interpretations as the story passes from one individual to another (any additions, subtractions, alterations, interpretations). You may want to use a recording form like the one found on page 26.

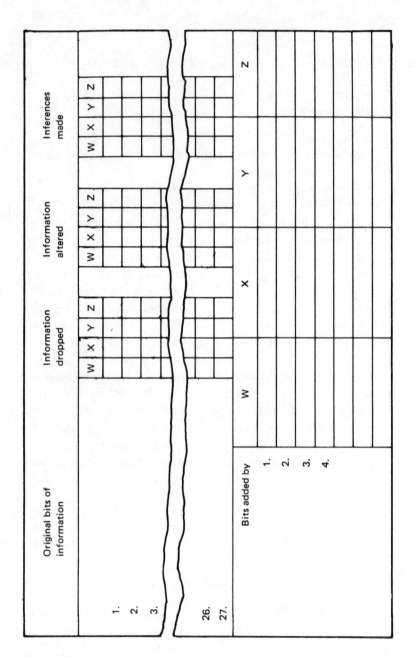

PANEL DISCUSSION

Panelists

Harold Johnson is Administrative Assistant III for the Department of Health Services, Mental Health Division, Los Angeles County. He holds an M.B.A., and he has taught business courses for two Los Angeles area colleges. Previously he worked as an operations analyst for Thrifty Drug Company and as a personnel analyst for Los Angeles County.

Carolyn A. Paulson recently moved to the East Coast and left her post as Manager of Industrial Relations for the CRYO-VAC Division of W. R. Grace & Co. She has been very active in civic affairs, and she is working on a graduate degree. Her current interests focus on organizational development through job design/enrichment studies and managerial development programs.

William D. Perreault is Vice President—Public Relations for Lockheed Aircraft Corp. He has been with various divisions of Lockheed for twenty years. Earlier he was in line management at Lockheed, and he once worked for American Airlines. For several years he served as Managing Editor of *American Aviation Magazine*.

Harold R. Riggins is Manager of the Corporate Telecommunications Department's Operations and Technical Support Section for Atlantic Richfield. He is also Vice President of ARCO Communications, Inc., a wholly owned subsidiary of Atlantic Richfield. He has held various posts in both the American Petroleum Institute and the Petroleum Industry Electrical Association.

Edward H. Rockey is Professor of Behavioral Science at the School of Business and Management at Pepperdine University. He has worked with several colleges, and has had various administrative posts, including divisional chairman, academic dean, and president. He earned his Ph.D. in Communications in Higher Education at New York University.

Edward H. Rockey

L to R: William D. Perreault, Carolyn A. Paulson, Edward H. Rockey, Harold Johnson, and Harold R. Riggins

Rockey: A manufacturing firm wouldn't entrust a valuable manufacturing process to an employee without determining that the employee understands something about the process. Too much money is at stake. I don't think a government agency or financial institution would turn over some vital system to an administrator without finding out how much the administrator knows about the system.

Every organization has interpersonal communication systems. They are not as visible as other kinds of systems, but they are there, and ultimately the efficiency of the organization is going to depend upon the effectiveness of those communication networks—formal and informal—because I don't think you can provide a service or product profitably or efficiently unless you have an effective communication pattern.

But most organizations seem to assume that anyone can communicate without organized thinking about communication or formal training. I don't think we test communication skills as much as some other kinds of skills, and so we turn over interpersonal communication networks, organizational communication networks, to managers without always determining the manager's knowledge of communication. What are some key problems in communication that you feel managers should know more about?

Perreault: I think the number one problem in organizational communication is *continuity*. We tend to communicate when we have an emergency, or a situation arises which we cannot avoid, and then we tell people what's going on. We do not communicate on a basis in which we have established a credibility and a confidence with the employee or with the organization. Nine out of ten of my management memos discuss changes in personnel. That's not what people are really interested in. They want to know what's going on in the company, how are things going with our customers, what are our fiscal problems, are they going to get raises, and so on.

Riggins: Another common problem is credibility. There is a credibility gap in most large organizations between your upper management and the worker or the middle management in that area. It comes out especially when you get into austerity programs, which we all go through from time to time. A good example of that is that everyone has to cut their budget 10 percent or whatever it is and you have to reduce people and activity. If you don't see management selling off any of the 30 airplanes that the company has, or something like that, and they are not traveling on commercial airlines; they're still flying around on private jets and all that kind of thing, then you create that credibility gap between the lower people and the upper people.

Paulson: The question is: Who is responsible? Who is the person who should be communicating to the employee? Should it be the immediate supervisor, the next level up, the president, the general manager?

Perreault: There's a tendency to say or refer to the management as "them" and to the workers as "us." Employees, particularly those that are unionized, are taught by the union management, "Look, those so-and-so's are looking out for themselves and we're looking out for us." And the result is, there is a constant vying, especially when you start to reduce personnel. We ended the year with about 27,000 people up here. Well, we had to reduce those 27,000 the first couple of months. You know that in the middle of the year there's going to be a couple more thousand laid off but you can't afford to go out and say there are going to be 4,000 people. It's true there are 2,000 laid off but there's going to be 2,000 more in June. There's no way you're going to approach that problem. There's a hundred and one interfaces, so you obfuscate in some variation. You talk about the amount of people who are going to disappear by attrition. It depends on what the order situation is and how our work load goes, but in June you're probably going to be laying off another 2,000 people. At that point in time that becomes a reality and they say, "Yeah, you remember what they said to us back in February," but in practical reality you can't tell a man in February that he's going to be gone in June. Because if you do, he's going to be a 20 percent worker or a 30 percent worker. In fact, if he's vindictive, he may go out there and exercise carelessness in the way he's doing his work. It's a big group when you're talking 2,000 or 3,000 people. There's a certain amount of those people, in any crowd that size—any cross-section that size—who are vindictive. It doesn't take much with an airplane or with almost any business. You cannot have total candor.

Johnson: Bill has indicated that you can't necessarily go tell all the truth you know, but some of the time key people within an organization ask the pointed question that is directly to the heart of it and get lied to. Facts come up later and credibility is destroyed forever.

Perreault: It depends on the level though. If you ask our chairman a direct question he's going to give you a direct answer. It may be that everybody in this organization has been told, "We mustn't say that sort of thing." His own sense of integrity is such that when he's asked it he's going to answer it and he's going to answer it very directly. But there is a problem in regard to the degree of candor and *who* is exercising that degree. You can't do it as an individual. You are trying to protect the system and you protect people also. Those are two-way streets.

Rockey: You talk about "obfuscating." I think it is "less worse" to hedge, and people know you're playing a game, than to deceive. I think that people can live with the fact that you're not going to tell something straight out. They sort of sense that, "Well, this is what we're going to try to do," and so on. They won't distrust you as they would if you tell them a falsehood and they find six months later that you have been deceiving them all along. Employees are mature enough to realize that managers are not going to tell the whole story every time.

Johnson: I have been put in that spot. Especially when it has been told me, as part of management, these are the facts, this is my recommendation on how we handle it, and I have gone to my work place and one of my subordinates has asked me, "What's going on?" or "What's going to happen?" and I have been as blunt as I can be and said, "I don't want to answer that question." Obviously, you know there is something behind my not wanting to answer it.

Perreault: General Abrahms, as the Chairman of the Joint Chiefs of Staff, had an expression which used to apply to generals who were going to testify before Congress. He always said, "Now give them the facts but don't blurt out the truth." It's cynical but it's tactful also. You can't, in fact, discuss with people all the facts all the time.

Rockey: What are some ways to reduce the problem of distortion in the chain of communication?

Perreault: Keep messages as brief as you can keep them, and keep them simple in their construction. As soon as I reach for the dictionary to make sure that that is the precise word I want, I realize I am making a mistake. If I have to examine whether or not that word says precisely what I want to communicate, I shouldn't be turning that loose on the employees. If I don't understand a word's precise meaning, I shouldn't be passing it on.

Johnson: We all make assumptions about people, and those assumptions have to be accurate, tied both to cultural and economic understanding. We really speak in several different languages and dialects within our work environment.

Rockey: How do we resolve this? I see a problem. What we are saying is the board of directors can't talk directly to the guy working at the machine, because of different languages. On the other hand, if the board tells the president, the president tells the V.P.'s and they tell the directors and they tell the managers, and they tell the supervisors, and the supervisors tell the guy working at the machine, we have a message interpreted and reinterpreted again and again.

Perreault: Tailor your communications. When we report our financial results we use something called a Form 10K. The Securities and Exchange Commission says you must report your year's operation. The 10K, I would say typically in our case, is 60 or 75 typewritten pages, with detailed technical language, of interest to a C.P.A. or an anti-trust division. We then take the Form 10K, and it's submitted and that's our official position with the government. We make that, and we have to put out the annual report. The annual report is going to have, I would say typically, 40 pages in it. That 40 pages will be half illustrations. And we will have taken out all of the detailed accounting background and how we did this and we'll show what the sales, the earning, the backlog, the equity, and so on and that's very good. But even in that group you're talking of going to that's what a financial analyst will use, that's what a stockholder who's informed will use, in fact, we have to tell the employees and we write a management memo and the management memo will probably be three pages. We write a news release that goes to the newspaper and it will probably be five pages. So we have these radiations of communications; so we are addressing the man at the level at which we expect his interest. We do that in most things. Some of them we do poorly. It depends on how much time we have and how much we recognize that the audience really is not technically literate. All of us are literate. We can read the newspaper, we can read a popular magazine, but in some disciplines we are not literate. We are not literate in organizational matters; we are not literate about technical problems; we are not literate about financial matters; we all have varying degrees of literacy, and I think the biggest mistake we make is that we assume that, "Well, the man can read" or, "The man is educated." So you have to adapt your message to his level of literacy in that discipline you're addressing him in.

Rockey: What is the effect on communication of confidence or lack of confidence in subordinates? The question as to whether they merit confidence is aside for the moment because that can go either way. What is the effect on communication flow, whether we are talking about vertical, up or down, horizontal, of confidence in people who report to us.

Riggins: I think if a manager instills complete confidence in his staff, his supervisors, his managers below him and so forth, and if he does that and does it honestly, you open the communication channel from this wide to this wide. I think you'll definitely increase the communications one hundred fold. That's my personal opinion. Now if you give the person the idea that you do not have confidence in him you are going to narrow it.

Johnson: Confidence has to be tested before it can be trusted. You know, I can trust you with anything until I find out, "Well, I'm not sure," and then self-preservation creeps in. I say, "Well, I have to go back to another dimension of me. My self-confidence has a great deal to do with how I trust you. I'm confident in myself. I can handle things and believe that you can because that's how I believe in myself." Under stress, back to the style again, we revert back to our natural being. You can't learn anything that makes you override, "When I get mad I lash out," and confidence goes to hell. I act inconsistent. The continuity of my behavior offsets the truth. When you get to the confidence level, when you trust and believe in people, I think you talk about an awful lot of dimensions that are not inherent to the work place but into our social lives.

Riggins: To establish confidence in this person, confidence in themselves, this in itself is a form of management, too. You have a job to do that you're delegating to a supervisor. You explain what you want done. The technique, at least that I use, I do not tell them how to do it. This is what we have to accomplish. In other words, you can drive a nail into a board with a hammer or you can drive it into a board with a rock, but the nail still gets in there and that's what I'm interested in. So you give them an assignment, let them run with it, and if they fall down you pick them up and pat them on the backside, tell them what they did wrong and send them on their way. Now if they did it right, then that's something that's out of the way. You no longer have to worry about anything else that comes up again in a repeat assignment of that type to that person. You have confidence in them. They know it and you pat them on the back and say, "You did a fine job."

Johnson: We're back to the coaching process, then.

Riggins: Right.

Paulson: This is a sure fire way of getting people developed but it's also very slow. It depends on your environment.

Perreault: I think basically that the confidence you have in people dictates the brevity of how much information you have to feed them. If I have a man and I say, "We're going to put out a release and we want to get this information to maximum, we want to get this to our usual audience," there is no question in my mind that he knows what that usual audience is. It means he is going to put that release into the business file which will go into all the editorial offices, and it means it will be hand delivered to the United Press and the Associated Press and in four or five cities to specific newspapers. I won't have to discuss with him what that means. I just say, "We want the maximum saturation on this."

That's the end of my discussion, because I understand he's been on that track. It's all engrained in him.

But, in fact, if I have a new man in here, and I give him a much broader set of instructions, then after I've given him the instructions almost invariably I get a gnawing feeling, "Does he really understand it?" I call him back and talk to him about two or three aspects that I'm certain about. The odds are great that I'm going to be back to him a third time because my own mind is sharpened—the focus is sharpened a little bit. I say, "I wonder if he thought of that?" I think there is a tremendous amount in the proved performance which says, "This man doesn't need a lot of guidance." That's why I communicate with him. I communicate to make sure that he's going to do what I want done.

Johnson: You know, I think that reminds me of something that happens with me. As a matter of fact I got an assignment yesterday evening that my boss's boss gave me. Normally, I get something, a piece of paper, with "take care of it" written at the bottom. Okay, I understand it. Respond to whomever it is, take care of whatever has to be done, put the right nuances in it and move on with it. This one came with "Prepare response for my signature." This tells me automatically: "Give me some backup data elsewhere. Make me a terse response to this, to that source, as you perceive it, but don't leave me out here with ten lines on a sheet of paper." When I give the response back it will probably have with it a page or a page and a half of backup data that says, "This is how I arrived at it. This is why it's in there that way. These are the things to avoid." I guess you could call it the staff work responsibility. I don't need, everytime I get an assignment, to hear, "Give me this information because I have to have it." I understand that.

Riggins: In a management position, I think that one of the biggest barriers in communicating with an employee, and on a one-to-one ratio, is that thing right there, or something similar to it, and that's that desk. That's just like a wall, in my opinion. In other words, if you have to talk and you're talking to one of your employees, and this is my own personal feeling now, if I should bring a man in for one reason or another—maybe he's in there for a dressing down—you can keep it at that, get up out of the chair and go over there and sit down.

Paulson: I wonder what Bill does? He's dealing on a colleague type of level. Do you often sit behind your desk?

Perreault: I almost invariably, if I can do it, I go to the man's place. I try to drop in and visit him. If there is any security to his area where I can talk to him without talking to a series of people, I try to go into his place and sit down. It's the same impact. He's really in the superior position. He's established in his surroundings. I spend most of my time in communicating in trying to establish a rapport: I have spent time as a short order cook; I've spent time as a mechanic; if I can talk and build some relationship and rapport, they know that I'm not sitting in an ivory tower or that if I am sitting in an ivory tower I have been through their channel and understand their problem. If I'm talking to educators I think of my career in education; whether it was an editor, which I consider educating people; whether it was as a salesman in aviation, which I feel is educating people about your airplanes which are complex structures. I try to establish the educator tie and go from there. In fact, as you say, if it is a man in the field I'd like to show him that I've been in the field. I try to do it with some direct tie with what he's doing—some intimate knowledge of what he's doing.

Riggins: In my case, I have about thirty people on the same floor that I'm located on in the tower, and I make it a point, oh, once a week, to drop in on a few each day, so I'll cover the whole group: Just sit down and say, "How is everything going today? Any problems?" We have that open type thing so it's not very private or anything like that. So you keep it on strictly a personal basis.

two

Listening in Organizations

OBJECTIVES

By applying the ideas in this chapter on listening, you should be better able to:

tune in on essentials
take helpful notes
extend listening range
resist distractions
receive messages accurately

Readers should also become more alert to the need to:

postpone judgment
reduce defensiveness
avoid one-upmanship
listen supportively
recognize emotional deafness
identify with speakers
have more interest in listening

For many years people have pondered over this question: "If a tree falls in the forest and no one hears it fall, does it make a noise?" We could debate this question for many more years without agreeing on an answer. But here is a more useful question, one we probably can find some agreement on: "If a member of an organization speaks and no one listens, has communication occurred?"

Suppose you typed an announcement and posted it on a bulletin board but not even one person ever saw it or read it, would you be communicating with that announcement? Hardly. In its essential definition, communication involves interaction. The term has the same root which appears in such words as "community," "communion," and "commune," all of which involve sharing or participation.

Up until quite recently communication training emphasized such sending skills as writing effective letters, making persuasive speeches, and leading successful meetings. But today *receptive* skills receive considerable attention, and courses in listening and reading appear more and more frequently.

This chapter explores two major areas which will help you improve your listening skills. You will find suggestions for specific steps you can take toward being a more effective listener, and you will read about attitudes which foster better listening.

KEY STEPS TOWARD MORE EFFECTIVE LISTENING

Fortunately, "listeners are made, not born." Experiments have demonstrated that listening behavior can improve. Just as we refine our writing and speaking habits, we can develop more productive listening habits. Whatever level of effectiveness in listening we may have already reached, the following suggestions will encourage continued growth.

Listen for the Essential Ideas

In every listening situation—conferences, telephone calls, speeches, interviews, and so on—we encounter more stimuli than we can absorb. We must tune in on the most vital issues. This usually requires selectivity, tuning out the irrelevant. Some of the speaker's comments may be merely introductory or illustrative or digressive. Usually supporting information will not be nearly as significant as the basic recommendations which it substantiates.

Possibly through repetition, through vocal emphasis, and through such statements as "but the most important issue is . . . ," the speaker will underscore the most significant points. This serves as one test of your listening skills: can you write down in a few crisp sentences the most important points the speaker has made?

Take Notes Productively

Experience has shown that certain ways of note-taking can make listening more productive. During various listening experiences—classes, lectures, training sessions, and so on—taking notes often helps in at least three ways: you provide a written record which you can use later for review; the act of writing helps you remember more of the material you heard; and you can write down suggestions and interpretations, ideas you might find useful later on but which you might forget if you did not record them immediately.

Effective note-taking does not involve slavishly copying every word or idea of a speaker. Surely we have all heard the story of the student whose class notes began, "Teacher entered classroom, put books on table and said, 'Good morning, class.'" Note only the most meaningful and useful information. Excessive note-taking may cause you to lose much of what the speaker says, break eye contact, or miss cues from other listeners.

Maintain flexibility in your note-taking style. For one situation, you may want to copy all key points; in another, you may choose to write down only action items. Experiment with a few different formats for taking notes. Some people find it helpful to leave a wide margin on the left for a summary or outline. This simplifies interpretation and re-

I. OVER BUDGET BY 6%	Staff Mtng. 4/11
	Overspending — First Quarter
	Storage fees 2,911.
	Supplies 4,917
	part time help 6,980.
	long dist. calls 860. *
	Cannot go over by more than 3% during this quarter.
II. POSSIBLE ECONOMIES	Brainstorming on some ways to cut back.
	— reduce inventory to lower storage fees.
	— fewer long distance calls. (use mail when possible)
	— tighten control on use of supplies. ✓

* ask Leslie about this.

✓ See if new requis. form is being used properly.

43

view. Some leave a space at the bottom of each page of notes for special comments or references (see page 43). As a standard for any method of taking notes, ask yourself, "Will this help me understand, remember, and act upon what the speaker is saying?"

Stretch Your Listening Muscles

Have you ever noticed a batter warming up during a baseball game? Does he swing an imaginary bat? No, he swings either two bats or a weighted bat. He tackles a challenge greater than the one at the plate. Perhaps this will build his confidence and strength and his ability to concentrate on the ball.

You can do something similar with regard to listening skills, and this exercise has become simpler in the age of tape recordings, especially the cassette type. Various companies produce recordings on topics which demand concentration—economics, politics, literature, selling, motivation, business, and so on. Many cassette tapes on such subjects are available free in the form of library loans. You can use a cassette player in your automobile and make commuting time profitable. You may want to make recordings of speeches you hear, and then compare the recording with your recollection or with your notes on the presentation.

Resist Distractions

Probably no human being can concentrate fully on one object, at least not for more than a second or two. (If you doubt this, try the first experiment in the "Skill Developers" section of this chapter.) So many stimuli surround us, and our attention tends to flit from one stimulus to another.

Effective listeners use several of the following techniques to stay tuned in on the speaker: (1) mantain an alert physical posture; (2) compare what you anticipated the speaker would say with what the speaker actually is saying; (3) review your notes; (4) concentrate on the structure of the presentation; and (5) observe the nonverbal cues of the speaker.

The difference between the speed of speech and the speed of thinking complicates the problem of distractions. Some people speak faster than others, but the average rate of speaking ranges between 150 and 180 words per minute; however, your "thought speed" is much faster. For example, a person who reads 500 to 800 words per minute will have quite a bit of "thinking room" left over when listening to a speaker who sends out only 160 words per minute.

By paying attention to all the suggestions in this chapter, you can use the extra "thinking room" productively and be a more effective listener.

KEY ATTITUDES FOR BETTER LISTENING

Accurate listening does not necessarily mean effective listening, and it may not lead to the fulfillment of such organizational goals as high morale, employee development, or optimum productivity. A clear example of sharp but unsupportive listening involves prosecuting attorneys. When a clever prosecuting attorney interrogates a defendant or a witness for the defense, keen listening may take place. The prosecutor watches every nonverbal cue, hears the vocal tones, weighs every word, notes details closely; but the motive behind this intense attention may be to trap and condemn the defendant. Thus a discussion of *supportive attitudes* becomes important in our discussion of listening.

A manager in an organization may listen to "trap" a subordinate, or to "prosecute" an employee. Similarly, a subordinate in an interview or staff meeting may hear only "incriminating evidence" against the boss. In horizontal communication, too, we may listen judgmentally to our peers.

Defer Judgment

It would be unrealistic and even unproductive to suggest that we should never make judgments with regard to what we hear, see, or read. Often an individual's job requires passing judgment on ideas or activities. In order for goals to be reached or wheels to be set in motion, we need someone to express approval or disapproval of plans or suggestions.

But the effective listener *defers* judgment until the facts are in, until an adequate hearing has taken place. Your internal conversation offers cues to help you discover the extent to which you defer judgment. Whenever we find ourselves hearing about a new idea and thinking, "That'll never work," we might ask ourselves, "Am I judging prematurely?" Have you ever sat in a meeting where someone presented a plan and before the speaker finished presenting the plan someone interrupted with such expressions as, "No way" or, "We tried something like that last year, and it was a bust?"

Sometimes at the opening of a committee meeting or staff session people think, "Well, here we go again; another dull meeting" or, "This is going to be a waste of time." Such judgments sometimes become self-fulfilling prophecies. We believe that the session will not benefit anyone; therefore, we don't listen attentively or respond helpfully, we don't hear anything worthwhile, and the meeting does turn out to be a waste of time.

Reduce Defensiveness

When we spend psychological energy defending ourselves, we tend to tune out what others say. As self-appointed defense attorneys, we try to secure a "not guilty" verdict for ourselves. If we think we're on trial, even valid information which might help us become more productive may be seen as incriminating evidence, which we must refute.

In an attempt to exonerate ourselves, we may fail to give others a fair hearing, and we may put others on the defensive. Two defensive people usually become two nonlisteners, each using words to both ward off attack and to strike back.

Self-defense is a natural instinct. Probably no human being could listen nondefensively with absolute consistency, but as we become aware of defensive nonlistening, and as we reduce defensiveness, we tend to listen more sensitively and accurately to what others say. It is equally important (see Chapter three of this text) to avoid putting others on the defensive.

Avoid One-upmanship

If we could record people's thoughts during discussions, how often would we find that while A was talking to B, B was not listening to A. Instead, B was thinking up a clever reply to A while A was talking; and perhaps what A was saying was a "put down," thought up while B was speaking earlier.

Of course, sometimes we must rebut. Sometimes others say things that are inaccurate, unwise, or unfair. But the likelihood of our reply being pertinent, logical, and fair-minded will depend in great part upon our care in listening effectively before we speak. The likelihood of getting a hearing will depend in large part upon whether other individuals feel that they are receiving a fair hearing.

Provide Supportive Attention

People who pay careful attention to what we say give us encouragement and respect. Such attention serves as a valuable form of nonverbal feedback: it says, "I am interested in you, in your problems, and in what you have to say right now. I value you as a person."

Listening to subordinates serves as an important example of this concept. Near the top of the list of coveted working conditions we find, "A boss who really listens to me." When the boss listens supportively, employees can develop confidence to participate with helpful suggestions, to provide important feedback, and to listen carefully in return when work is delegated or policies are handed down.

Recognize Your Emotional Deafness

Can you identify some subjects you tune out, some topics you "just don't hear?" All of us exercise both *selective perception* and *selective exposure.* Selective perception means that we see and hear what we need to see and hear, what we expect to see and hear, and what we want to see and hear. But selective exposure means that we expose ourselves only to selected messages. A good example of this occurs during election campaigns. Except for those rare individuals who show vital interest in understanding many points of view, most of us tend to ignore the issues and candidates we oppose. We subscribe to newspapers and magazines which support our candidate, and we ignore editorials, columns, and radio and television programs which support the opposition.

Emotional deafness may relate to traditional concepts: "Who ever heard of a woman who could do that job?" It may express our racial prejudices: "You can't trust 'one of them.'" It may reveal our occupational stereotypes: "They are all engineering (or accountant or police or production) types." It may expose our partisan loyalties: "Management will never understand" or "Labor will never understand." In such cases, because of emotional deafness, we don't allow certain messages to get through to us.

Emotional deafness will probably never disappear; apparently it's a permanent and universal malady. But we can recognize our own emotional deafness, and attempt to listen with a more open mind. When we do, we often hear things that "just weren't there before."

Be a Selfish Listener

A trainer once impressed me with his openness and self-awareness and honesty. He told a group, "You know, I've noticed one thing about myself. Usually I don't get turned on unless there's a definite payoff for me. . . ." He then told us what he considered a payoff. But the important issue in connection with effective listening is not his payoff but yours. Identify the rewards you seek and find the connection between what you want and what or whom you are listening to.

Perhaps you seek recognition from your boss. You might ask yourself, "As I listen to my superior, how can I perceive more accurately what the boss wants me to do?" Perhaps you seek a promotion. "How will these ideas further my career?" Perhaps you desire to perform creatively or more productively. "How can I use this information to complete this task successfully?" Ask whatever questions you must in order to get in touch with your motivations and with the connection between the words being spoken and your motivations.

Be Ready to Restate

Could you restate what the preceding speaker has just said, to that speaker's satisfaction? If you have the willingness and courage to do that, you have come a long way as a listener.

Total understanding of another person's communications may be impossible, but understanding increases when we are willing to summarize what we heard. The need for this practice becomes obvious when people attempt it: quite often the person whose message is summarized will say, "But that's not quite what I meant." So the listener tries again, as the first speaker repeats what was meant in the first place. Even then, after a second attempt to summarize, the original speaker may say, "Well, you're closer; you've almost got it."

Empathize

In order to be able to restate the feelings and thoughts of others, we must first exercise the imagination and identification required. We must cultivate the capacity to see things from the other person's point of view, to put ourselves in the other person's position.

Apparently, some people avoid experiencing empathy because they confuse it with agreement. They experience fear of change or "conversion," so they resist identifying with the other person's problem. But empathic listening does not necessarily require acceptance of the views of others. It does lead to understanding what others mean.

While carrying a floral wreath to a gravesite, a Westerner noticed an Oriental placing a bowl of rice on a tomb. In a rude stage whisper, the Westerner exclaimed, "I wonder if he thinks his dead friend will come alive and eat that rice;

seems silly to me." The Oriental heard this and replied, "Perhaps my ancestor will rise and eat this rice . . . the same day that your ancestor rises and smells those flowers." Empathy would require neither sympathy for the loss of the other mourner nor the willingness to adopt the other person's mode of honoring the dead; however, empathy would cause us to say, "Given a certain heritage—a family, a nationality, a culture, a religion—a bowl of rice could be a sensible, beautiful tribute. Given a different heritage, a floral piece could be a sensible, beautiful tribute. If I were of a different background, a practice which now seems strange would seem familiar, fitting, and natural."

In organizations we work with people representing various loyalties, backgrounds, interests, and occupations. To listen effectively, we must cultivate the capacity to put ourselves in the other person's place, to see things from the other person's point of view. This identification will help us to understand more deeply. We may discover that we agree with the other person. On the other hand, we may find that, even after empathic listening, we disagree; but if we do disagree, the other person will sense our effort to see his or her point of view. Probably the other person will either accept "No" more readily or some reasonable compromise will follow. In any event, if we disagree, we will tend to disagree without being disagreeable, knowing that each person has made a real effort to understand the other.

CONCLUSION

Listening influences all of the functions of organizational efficiency and leadership. Successful planners or innovators must be open to suggestions and new ideas. When delegating responsibility we must listen in order to ascertain that employees understand the assignment; in receiving orders we must listen carefully so that we know what we are expected to do. Those who represent organizations must be alert to what various publics and internal groups think about policies and actions. In organizing groups, we must listen to feedback in order to learn how the structure affects morale and productivity. In staffing, we must learn quite a bit about prospective employees by listening to them.

Imagine a grievance-handling session in which one representative talks for twenty minutes and then says, "Well, I've told you *our* side of the story; now let me tell you *their* side." Absurd as this may sound, we sometimes behave as if we know both sides of an issue and have no need to listen to the other point of view. For another example of non-listening, suppose the representative said, "Well, I've told you my side of the story, and now I'm leaving because I don't want to hear or understand the other side." Sometimes we behave in such a way that others conclude that we will not listen and don't care to understand.

Communication in organizations improves when listening improves. Effective listening is more than a personal skill involving certain steps and attitudes. Effective listening affects morale and efficiency, organizational impact, and productivity.

SKILL DEVELOPERS

1. To learn something about human patterns of attention, try this experience in concentration. Attempt to concentrate totally on one object for ten seconds. If you choose a visual experiment, select one physical object

(your right index finger will do). See it alone, and note no other stimuli for ten seconds. Most individuals will note several other stimuli intruding during the first few seconds of the experiment.

2. During a family (or class, work, or social) disagreement offer to restate what the preceding person has just said, and check for confirmation from them. What happened?

3. Purchase or borrow some educational tapes. Practice listening for longer and longer periods of time.

4. Keep a communications log for at least one day. Which activity absorbed the most time? Enter the number of minutes in the appropriate columns.

Time	Listening	Speaking	Writing	Reading
8:00 AM				
8:15 AM				
8:30 AM				
8:45 AM				
9:00 AM				
9:15 AM				
etc.				

PANEL DISCUSSION

Rockey: Carolyn has a statement on "effective listening."

Paulson: I believe there has been a trend toward the development of listening skills, at least on the management level, as
much emphasis in that area as human relations behavior and
effective time utilization. Listening is in three distinct areas:
fact, feelings, and fantasy. The ability to listen is keyed to a
person's ability to listen actively, objectively, analytically,
with empathy, and to utilize all your senses, reviewing nonverbal and verbal communication for consistency.

I believe that the development of listening skills within
an organization tends to resolve a couple of problems. I
think it facilitates the identification of key issues very rapidly when you're listening for feelings of fact and fantasy. I
believe that it facilitates creative problem solving and it will,
in the long run, create a more efficient and smoothly-running
operation. A commitment to developing good listening skills
is based on management's commitment toward developing
what I consider to be good objectives and goals. I think there
should be a long-range planning effort, and I believe that
there should be intermediate short-range planning efforts
that accompany that. These are complemented by reasonable
goals and timetables. There is a factor in wanting to increase
effectiveness in an organization which is pure economics,
linking economics with the ability and effectiveness of communication systems within the organization, employment
stability, the rate of absence and the absenteeism cost, improved interpersonal relationship, very basically, the reduc-
tion of anxiety in an employee which facilitates better working relationships and interpersonal contacts, the ability to
communicate. That creates in and of itself an accountability
factor: if my boss is willing to listen to me, if I have a feeling
of what is expected of me and I know what measurement
standards I am being judged by, then I am more apt to take
personal responsibility for my job; I am more apt to make

Carolyn A. Paulson

William D. Perreault

independent decisions and probably develop mentally over the long run and proceed a lot further.

As I stated before, I think the ability to develop good listening skills is keyed into two or three very basic aspects. One, the development of good objectives and goals with reasonable guidelines. I think that people expect their leader to lead and that they are looking to that individual to lead the ship. Once those wheels are set into action and good behavioral concepts are applied to the management of people, you seem to find a better environment. That, of course, is coupled with the feedback system. I haven't determined in my mind whether you establish good objectives and goals and then feedback systems or you work the other way around. You establish the goals and behavioral concepts fit in there and then you get the feedback systems. Maybe there are two kinds of feedback systems. What I'm primarily talking about is the measurement of what an individual is doing, what he or she thinks that they should be doing, and how they are measured by those standards. I believe that people, generally, perceive the organization to be what they think it is. It is important to establish the climate of constructive and positive attitudes and working relationships, that people will work within that framework. They do not necessarily have to be told that, "Your job as a PBX Receptionist demands that you dress well and act in a cordial and friendly manner." I think they do that automatically if they know what the job is.

Without going into all that I have prepared and all the information which is tied to it, I came across an interesting fact, and I'm not sure where I picked it up. Most of us spend 60 percent of our day listening and we forget 30 to 50 percent of what we hear in an eight-hour period of time. That's pretty startling, when we think that managers spend 90 percent of their time communicating. I have communications problems and I'm sure people don't hear me and I don't hear what they're saying a lot. Someone has said, "The problem is not one of getting people to talk. The problem is getting leaders to listen." That's generally how I feel about improving communications and listening skills within the organization.

Johnson: When wild stallions lead a herd, you see them run with their head turned, they find out where the bulk of the animals are, and they turn, proportionate to saying, "I've got to now shift the weight of my following to the avenue that I want to take." He just doesn't run blind like, "Follow me." They don't follow exactly either, but if there are too many to the right it would tend to make them drift off in the wrong direction. So he swings right to get in front again.

Riggins: I noted briefly from the previous conversation, that I sometimes wonder if enough emphasis is placed on hearing with the eyes. I feel that you get as much out of watching people when they're speaking to you as you do actually listening.

Rockey: How can you be confident that you have been listening adequately, effectively?

Paulson: I try to say, "What I hear you saying is. . . ." If I get it right I get confirmation, and if I get it wrong I get an explanation.

Johnson: I get a more secure feeling about how I have listened if a day, a week, a couple of days later, I go back to the same person, especially where a problem had existed. I am curious as to, "did we resolve that?" I take the feedback initiative, that I'm still interested. Everything that is said isn't closed; let's talk about it.

Rockey: I hear Carolyn saying, "Get confirmation from the other person that you understand what they said." Harold, you're saying, "Be available. Continue the dialogue."

Johnson: We've had a discussion about something. During the night something clicks. I am not comfortable with that.

I'll come back the next day and say, "I'd like to talk about this. I had this feeling. Is that really what you were saying? Is that what you intended?" Project that I'm sincerely concerned about the problem, so it doesn't get out of hand.

Paulson: You can tell when someone is upset. I think that it is pretty apparent, particularly to managers. I think we are sensitized to people and how things are going. We can tell by mannerisms what is going on—even the most subtle mannerisms. I learned a very interesting lesson last year. I traveled a lot. My group was beginning to demonstrate to me, in a lot of various ways, that they felt I wasn't available. I just finally said to my boss, "I am not going to travel any more. These are the problems that I see, and I'm going to stay home for a couple of months." One of them just came to me last week and said there was a fantastic change, and how much more comfortable they were. They had been thinking about leaving. It was a matter of, "I never could see you, and if you were there, people were with you." The availability thing is very important. Even if they never come in, they have the option to come in.

Rockey: What sort of cues do you get from people who you consider very effective listeners? You mentioned something about their eye contact . . .

Riggins: Yes, that's a very major thing. As a matter of fact I have a little bit of a problem with someone in my company. To be absolutely honest with you, I'll be in there talking to him and he might be suddenly staring out the window and I'm not sure he's listening to me. Actually, he might be listening but I'm not sure he is hearing.

Rockey: We look for nonverbal attentiveness cues—eye contact, not being involved in distractions, shuffling drawers, answering phones . . .

Perreault: I gauge my listening by my questioning. If I can sit and listen to a man talk for an extended period and not ask the man some probing questions about some of the things he is saying, then I feel that I am not listening. I feel I'm not with it. I don't know how an intelligent mind can listen to a person who has either a real or imagined problem and have them ramble on for a long time and not ask some perceptive questions in the area, though one has to be careful not to block the man's line of thinking, to intercept him and to frustrate him by questions.

Rockey: If the other person asks alert, bright, pertinent questions, we have something sinking in and stimulating them not only to get what we're saying but wanting to know more about it and to focus on those particular aspects that are most meaningful.

Perreault: I was a reporter for some time. When I used to go and ask questions of a man and he would be garrulous or he would ramble, no matter what subject I asked him; information would ramble out and I would generally try to question without notebook and without recording. Then I would start to take notes in some depth. Suddenly the man would appreciate that it was being recorded, and it was making an impression; his tone changed. He would start thinking seriously, "I'm about to wind up in print with this." I feel that this is the other side of the same question.

Riggins: Another debatable method of assuring yourself that you are listening or hearing; that is the interruption method. When you are speaking with someone and he is giving a long dissertation, ask, "Excuse me, But do I understand you correctly at this point?" This, then gives that person the feeling, "Yes, he is definitely listening to me or he would not be stopping me here before I went further."

Rockey: One other question on listening. What do you perceive are the most acute listening problems in vertical communication; upward and/or downward? Let's say,

someone is delegating; what would most likely be the subordinate's listening problem? Someone is giving a grievance
or giving feedback to management. What is management's
listening problem going to be?

Perreault: I view management's listening problem as the
subordinate's tendency to feel we have to describe how to
"build a watch" in detail. If I go to my management and
say, "Look, I'm having a problem in this area." They want
to know that problem. But principally, they want to know
two or three sentences worth of it or a couple of paragraphs
worth of it. If I'm going to give him all the gory details of
it, he is going to be very impatient and he is going to fidget
and by the time I get to the point he is wondering, "What
do you propose? What do you want from me?" Normally,
my management wants to participate when, in fact, there
is a reason for making a decision—if they can help me, if
they can give me authority, if they can do something like
that. If I want to go in and tell them all my problems they
couldn't be less interested, and I turn them off very rapidly.
I think that the issue in communicating upward is to make
it brief. Preferably, ask for an authority that you don't have
or propose a solution that you feel you want their answer
to. Even in the solution; make it brief. Don't tell them all
the gore of how you're going to do it, all the personalities,
all the problems it creates.

Johnson: Present the problem. Make it brief. Establish it in
your mind before you get there, and have it organized; what
do you think should happen; give a supporting rationale.
Usually you get the whole problem: "How do you make the
watch?" rather than, "The watch isn't working, and I want
to put in a mainspring."

Perreault: My present boss says, when I go in to tell him the
obvious, "I know that." He wants to know, "What is new here?
What do you want from me?"

Rockey: In terms of management listening to subordinates and subordinates listening to management, are there different types of defensiveness? When would management be listening and be defensive? When would subordinates be listening and be defensive and it would be a problem to listen well?

Johnson: Criticism makes defensiveness, regardless of which way it goes.

Rockey: Criticizing the company or criticizing the employee?

Johnson: No matter what.

Perreault: I feel that your management has to feel comfortable with you. You know that the management is the boss. The management, at any level, is never quite that secure. They might be in a moment of anger where they respond without reason. But basically, I feel that the management wants to feel comfortable. If they have twelve people in a room and everytime they go into that room the head of Industrial Relations has a habit of pressing them on the basis of, "You just don't understand the situation out here with the employees," or, "Don't you read the papers? Haven't you noticed what has been going on over at Convair in the same area?" or, "Don't you know that they're trying to unionize the engineers somewhere?" You might take that once. If each time you go into a room to gather and he feels, "What is that fellow going to do to embarrass me today," pretty soon he has a new fellow in there. He doesn't want to be put on the offensive. He doesn't want to feel uncomfortable. If he is comfortable with you, he listens to your ideas; he feels he can accept or reject them and it isn't what you say but it is an attitude as though, "This poor jerk doesn't understand the problem." A lot of junior people do that to you.

Johnson: I told a superior one day about a problem that he took issue with. I expressed, "You evidently are naive." I'll never do that again. He said, "After 25 years in the same damn building, you tell me I'm naive. Let me tell you who hired you."

three

Management Style and Communication

OBJECTIVES

Readers should develop a keener awareness of how the following affect communication:

> authority
> punishing
> hoarding information
> decision making
> dogmatism
> adult-adult transactions
> checking on people
> giving pep talks

"Now are there any questions or comments?" the manager asked at the close of the weekly staff meeting. No. As usual, no comments, no questions. The manager had already "said it all," as far as the employees were concerned. Despite the request for comments or questions from the boss, what the employees really heard went something like this: "I've just asked for questions or comments; however, you know a few things about me: if you do ask a question, either I'll humiliate you here or clobber you later. I don't really want any comments; that's why I waited until two minutes before the end of the meeting to ask for them. Comments would infer that I haven't said all there is to be said on the subject, and I have."

Fortunately, few situations are that bad. But communication between the boss and his or her subordinates is usually more restricted than the boss thinks, even in the best of circumstances. In a study reported by Likert,[1] 34 percent of

[1] Rensis Likert, "Motivational Approach to Management Development," *Harvard Business Review*, July–August 1959, p. 78.

the subordinates surveyed agreed that their supervisor understood their problems; however, 95 percent of their supervisors thought they understood their subordinates problems
well—a 61 percent "communication gap"!

Consider another staff meeting, quite unlike the previous
one. The boss doesn't often ask for questions or comments
formally, but discussion flows freely during the course of the
meeting. The style of the leader seems to say, "You may ask
questions at any time. I welcome your comments. I respect
you and your viewpoints." Fortunately, most of us have
been in meetings characterized by meaningful dialogue and
full participation. In any case, the leadership style has a
strong influence on the communication flow.

AUTHORITY AND COMMUNICATION PATTERNS

The effects of leadership styles on communication start very
early. The typical pre-school child knows much about authority and communication. Such a youngster may never have
heard of such terms as "horizontal communication" or "vertical communication" or "message adaptation," but the child
has practiced all of these.

A three-year-old may call a friend "Marie," but Mother's
sister must be called "Aunt Marie." A four-year-old might
say to a two-year-old, "Give that to me, or else!" However,
when making a similar request of Father, the sentence will
probably begin with something like, "Dad, please may I
have. . . ."

If we recorded and studied all the conversations in one
day at a nursery school, we would probably note some interesting differences among expressions directed toward close
friends compared with those directed toward teachers or
toward very dominant or very passive children. Young chil-

dren do not discuss such formal questions as organizational charts, lines of authority, hostile grapevines, pecking orders or hidden agendas, but most children have experienced these, have experimented with them, and have formed appropriate response patterns. Children manipulate such communication aspects as physical distance, tone of voice, choice of words, types of gestures, timing, facial expressions, and vocal volume. Very significantly, they also make adjustments in the topics to be discussed and in the disclosure or nondisclosure of information. Often the manipulation of all these, have experimented with them, and have formed apother hand, it may occur very deliberately. A good example of the latter with an authority figure involves a teacher or parent who says: "Now go over there and stay by yourself, and when you're ready to talk nicely you can go out and play."

Obviously communication patterns differ among families and schools, and leadership patterns have much to do with the variations. Consider these two extremes. In one family, almost "anything goes." Short of danger to life and limb or interfering painfully with the rights of others, children feel free to do what they want and to say what they want. In another family, "children are to be seen and not heard." Even a disrespectful tone of voice will bring a clout on the head and loss of privileges. Without evaluating the parental styles involved with regard to morality or child-rearing theories, imagine the differences in openness regarding vertical communication upwards.

Imagine a nursery school which encourages the children to participate in decisions about procedures, to make recommendations for activities, and to question the teachers' viewpoints and methods. In another school, teachers and administrators make all the decisions and students frequently hear, "Do as you are told." Again, without debating educational theories, imagine the differences regarding the flow of information upwards as well as the content of horizontal communication.

Similarly, leadership styles in work situations have much to do with communication patterns, and the main goal of this chapter is to examine such styles and patterns.

COMMUNICATION AND LEADERSHIP BEHAVIOR

This section identifies specific behaviors of organizational leaders and some communication patterns associated with those behaviors. Readers may associate most of these behaviors with various theories of management; however, this book does not pretend to serve as an analysis or explanation of such theories. It does focus on the application of the leader's conduct to communicating effectively in organizations. This book does not pretend to analyze or explain various psychological theories which readers may associate with the behaviors discussed. It does center on how an individual's acts may affect organization communication.

To Clobber or Not to Clobber

Leaders possess fate control. Managers make recommendations regarding promotions or raises. Officers make decisions about requests for transfer. Administrators approve expenditures. Supervisors control such things as work space and vacation dates. Directors must sanction some executive decisions.

When a subordinate interacts with a superior in an organization, no matter what the personal relationship or the line authority, the consciousness of fate control persists. At worst, the boss can punish vindictively. At best, the boss can discipline constructively. As the saying goes, "Punishment is administered for the sake of the one giving it; discipline for the sake of the one receiving it."

In any event, the boss has whack, and the exercise of power in a disciplinary way will influence communication. One of the realities of organizational life involves the power authorities must have in order to affect decisions and achieve results. The manner in which the power is used will affect communication.

A Punishing Style

In Washington, D.C., new legislators receive a proverb from some seasoned ones: "If you want to get along, go along." Whatever virtue this saying may have, if any, it obviously tends to intimidate, and to restrict dialogue: "If you speak out against proposals, you'll end up a social outcast." Dissent seems to mean disloyalty, and disloyalty brings a kind of punishment.

Some managers, supervisors, and administrators come across as coercive: "Agree with me or I'll clobber you." Subordinates may perceive nonconformist views or counter suggestions as unpopular or even dangerous. Under such circumstances very little feedback will come to the coercer except "O.K." or "Whatever you say." The boss will be out of touch with employees' views and suggestions.

When subordinates who work in coercive situations make mistakes, instead of going to the boss, admitting the error, and asking for corrective help, they may avoid contact with the boss. Probably they will try to cover up the mistake, and this often costs the organization time, material, and money.

Reducing Threats

While it seems unrealistic to think that an authority figure would never exercise fate control, some leaders seem more accepting of human error, more tolerant of mistakes, and more apt to make specific suggestions to remedy the situation, rather than make accusations or hurl threats. When people report to this type of leader, they may more readily acknowledge mistakes and get help.

People who report to a boss who reduces threats may feel freer to make counter proposals, and these may result in increased efficiency. The boss may receive more feedback about management style, and this may offer the boss opportunity for personal growth and organizational advancement. More creative dialogue may evolve in staff meetings, resulting in greater organizational effectiveness.

"I Know Something You Don't Know"

Access to information tends to accompany power in organizations. The more information one has, the more prestige one enjoys, particularly when the information is strategic. Organizations often restrict some information, and with good reason, to key people. But some information may pass officially through the entire organization, reaching literally everyone (across-the-board pay increases, new regulations involving all employees, and so on). Some information passes unofficially through the entire organization, reaching literally everyone.

Hoarding Information Needlessly

In an apartment house in Southern California a tenant secretly carried boxes of rocks into his apartment. When he disappeared and the owners gained access to the apartment, they discovered tons of rocks piled high in boxes throughout the apartment. The rocks seemed to have no value.

In organizations people sometimes file away information, getting some sort of secret pleasure by keeping it from

co-workers or subordinates (or even from superiors!). Sometimes, as time passes, the value of all this old information can
be something like the worth of that pile of rocks—nothing.
Meanwhile, many people may feel left out, and stranded on
the fringe of the communication network. They will tend to
resent the hoarder and to start their own secret "pile of
rocks."

Sharing Unclassified Information

Organizations go to great lengths to keep in touch with
various publics—government agencies, clients, and so on. But
often company news affects employees more than any public. People want to feel included, informed, and aware. Two
key organizational benefits may accompany the sharing of
information about such matters as future changes, new products or services, and various "larger issues" of the organization: (1) employees may feel more significant, more involved
in the future of the organization; and (2) employees may
offer more feedback and more suggestions regarding the
direction of the organization.

When Leaders Make Decisions

The decisions made by first-level supervisors vary con-
siderably from the decisions made by top management. As
people receive more and more responsibility in organizations, the weight of decision making becomes heavier. As
with so many topics in this chapter, decision making is a
complex subject about which many books have been written,
but we are concerned here with a limited question: what
effects do decision-making styles have upon communication?

"Here's What You're Gonna Do"

According to the Old Testament, even Jehovah considered

advice. Moses and Abraham made suggestions and negotiated, and Jehovah adopted plans. But some managers out-mighty the Almighty; they don't want advice from anyone. They come across as isolated decision makers who want to be left alone, even though this pattern may tend to produce less effective decisions and to cut off the flow of suggestions and creativity.

Involving People in Decisions

We tend to support what we help to create. We tend to cooperate with output when we've had a chance for input. Of course leaders must accept responsibility for decisions. "The buck stops here" appeared on the desk of President Truman. But arrangements can be made for a flow of ideas and information to the person who has to make the decision, and in some cases team decision making can function successfully. In either case, when people feel included in decisions they are more likely to contribute, to implement, and to engage in productive discussions.

Dogmatism or Dialogue?

Human beings have struggled for centuries over questions of knowing, certainty, and finality. Uncertainty has been so threatening to some people that they have isolated or even killed people who have expressed doubt. Without trying to philosophize deeply about degrees of knowing, we often observe how degrees of dogmatism affect patterns of discussion.

"And That's Final!"

Yes, finality can be final, and when the boss slams the door (literally or figuratively), discussion ceases. As indicated at the beginning of this chapter, subordinates will clam up

when they perceive the boss sending out signals of infalli-
bility and finality. Some writers have used the term "allness"
to describe this situation. Allness seems an apt choice, for
some people appear to have "said it all."

When someone gives the impression that the last word
has been said, how much room is left for comments, questions, or suggestions? Further discussion may be perceived
as disloyalty, threat, or rebellion. Of course, allness doesn't
afflict only bosses. Co-workers and subordinates may indicate
that they have made up their minds absolutely and un-
changeably. Such people will not often receive advice or
questions from peers, and (unless they have unusual job
security) they may find themselves transferred or fired by
their superiors.

The "Etc." Person

ETC. might seem an odd title for a magazine, yet the
International Society for General Semantics publishes one
with that title. On the front page of each issue a justifica-
tion for the title appears, written by Alfred Korzybski for the
first issue of the publication:

> ... we do not assume that what we say can cover all the
> characteristics of a situation, and so we remain conscious
> of a permanent *et cetera* instead of having the dogmatic,
> period and stop attitude.

This tentativeness, this openness can be transmitted nonverbally by a tone of voice, an attitude, or a pause which
gives the other person an opportunity to offer feedback. It
may be transmitted verbally through such comments as, "Of
course, there must be some way to accomplish this that we
haven't even thought of yet" or, "I wonder what additional
data we haven't considered."

While dogmatists exchange monologues, duets of the
psychologically deaf, people who leave room for other

ideas and new concepts tend to get into dialogues. Instead of being contests to make one person right and the other wrong or speechless, conferences and interviews can become opportunities for growth and shared insights.

How Are Your Transactions Lately?

Through such books as *I'm OK; You're OK* or *Born to Win* most of us have heard about such transactions as Child-Parent and Adult-Adult. Communication patterns are influenced by the types of transactions we enter into, and these transactions occur in formal organizations as well as in families and informal social groups.

Nurturing Dependent Employees

When a supervisor comes across as a nurturing parent, a number of employees will probably respond as dependent children. Some leaders seem to think, "If I don't protect 'my people,' who will? They look to me for guidance and protection, and they won't survive or produce unless I keep them under my wing." Such a leader will often end up with a whining brood of employees who constantly and needlessly ask for help. The communication pattern will probably be: overburdening the boss with frequent questions and pleas for advice; very little clear delegation of responsibility; and excessive need for praise and reassurance.

Encouraging Adult-Adult Conversations

The dependent question, "What should I do?" may be met with the response, "What information do you have, and which way do you think you should go?" The Adult in each of us tends to focus on processing data objectively, keeping in touch with what is real, organizing our thought rationally, accepting responsibility for ourselves, allowing others to be responsible for themselves and taking a clear-headed look at the consequences of our actions. Each of us has a capacity to exercise this Adult within us, and to interact with others from that ego state. Adult-Adult transactions may lead to such communication patterns as: clearly delegating responsibility; accepting responsibility; calmly discussing likely outcomes; sharing relevant information; and reducing and recognizing prejudices, opinions, and "hang-ups."

This does not mean that the leader never expresses sympathy or never takes time out for fun. It does mean that the general pattern of communication encourages others to grow, to accept responsibility, and to be independent.

To Check or Not to Check

Managers must measure results and evaluate productivity. Without such control organizations would not function efficiently. But the style of the person checking will affect communication.

Frequently Checking on People

The checker-upper may come across as someone who thinks, "If I don't personally look in on people often, they make mistakes. In fact, if I didn't watch them, they might not do any work at all." People subjected to "over the shoulder" scrutiny may feel, "My boss doesn't trust me, and I don't trust people who don't trust me. Very little confidence is shown in my initiative."

When people feel constantly under surveillance, communication may be guarded and clouded with resentment. Though the words themselves may be civil, employees will really be saying to the boss, "Get lost!"

Controlling Without Peeking Over the Shoulder

Results can be measured without constantly checking on

people. Several years ago I worked as a deck hand on the Erie Canal. On one voyage we had a first mate who had gone to sea fifty years earlier, on a wooden sailing ship, when he was a teenager. He attempted to transfer his nineteenth-century sailing ship style to us, and it didn't work. Sometimes when he appeared to watch us work, we would stare back at him, and he would become even more abrupt and grumpy than usual. On one watch, when he was in charge of the vessel, we ran aground. We stayed there for a couple of days, and it cost the steamship company quite a bit of money to solve the problem. If the first mate had spent more time studying his charts, while delegating more supervision to a bosun, the accident might not have occurred. Instead of looking over our shoulders, he should have been looking over his plans for the vessel. He could have checked on results rather than on minute-by-minute progress.

To Pep or Not to Pep

Communication and motivation are closely related. In some organizational relationships we find people who think that by telling others how they should feel, what they should think, and what they should do, motivation will take place. In other situations we find individuals who assume that each person is self-motivated and that we cannot motivate another person.

Giving Pep Talks

Some leaders think that there is a direct correlation between pep talks and productivity. "Pepper-uppers" may perform at staff meetings, over the telephone, in interviews, or through memos.

People who work for a "pepper-upper" may begin to feel like voice-activated tape recorders; they don't work unless

someone else is talking; they are not self-starters, since someone else must push the button and get things moving. Why
should such objects initiate? Why should they enter into
dialogue? After the "pepper-upper" has administered the
verbal adrenalin for the day, what is left for the receiver
to say?

Suggesting and Listening

Most people will more readily talk a problem through and
contribute to the solution when they have the opportunity
to engage in meaningful dialogue. When people are lectured
to, they may feel that they are the problem.

CONCLUSION

Attitudes and relationships have much more influence on
communication than do techniques or formats. When inter-
actions are characterized by trust, respect and confidence,
people talk and listen more maturely, more openly, and more
constructively. When people feel put down, excluded or
threatened, communication patterns may become defensive,
sullen, or retaliatory. Regardless of media investments or
communication policies, the personal styles of managers
will have the greatest influence upon the quality of organizational communication.

SKILL DEVELOPERS

1. Here are three role-playing experiences. You may work

with these on your own, but you may find it more interesting to experiment with them in small groups.
a. During a problem-solving staff meeting, someone makes a suggestion. Your first impression is that the plan won't work, but you want to avoid the "That'll never work" type response. You want to avoid squelching or threatening the suggestor. What can you ask or state to contribute productivity to a dialogue on the suggestion?
b. You have delegated a responsibility to an individual, but this individual keeps coming back to you, asking for help in fulfilling the task. Simulate the possible reactions you might have. (Various students may participate in the dialogue by rotating in the roles of supervisor and subordinate.)
c. You are conducting a review session for a subordinate. On several points you are pleased with the employee's performance, but on a few areas of performance you want to see improvement during the next six months. With various students rotating as interviewer and interviewee, simulate the discussion.
2. Analyze your conversations with peers, superiors, and subordinates. What differences do you note?
3. Describe your communication patterns when you feel defensive, threatened, squelched, or hostile.

PANEL DISCUSSION

Johnson: I think it is kind of difficult to talk about communications and supervisors, especially at the line level, without addressing the negatives. In my observation and exposure, skills in communication of most line-level supervisors are substandard. I think that they are substandard for a number of different reasons. Among them, that few people have ever been prepared for the role of supervisory communication. You grow up becoming a technician. You condition yourself for getting the job done and effectively reporting how well you've done it or the detail of it. You never really address yourself to that problem of, "How do I tell someone else how effectively they have done it?" Supervisors are balancing their scales for communicating with subordinates, primarily to deal with problems. They don't generally speak much to the excellence of performance of other people, except finding fault, and it erodes the base on which they can communicate effectively. If every time I've ever heard a comment from a superior, I've had negatives, I have no faith in them bringing anything about how well I do things. Subsequently, I don't try too hard to perform with excellence.

Counseling is normally spoken of in terms of negatives. People counsel about behavioral problems in the sense that, "You have done poorly at something, and that's too bad, and we're going to have to make modifications there." There's little of the coaching effect of, "Let me help you develop a skill. Let me talk to you as a friend. Let me help you understand the necessity, the importance, the ease of all of our activity so that we can approach our work and our understanding in a more wholesome manner," including, "May I take the responsibility for clarifying our understandings in our view of each other?"

Some supervisors have a problem with not being permitted or not being provided with a private location in which to discuss matters, whether personal, job related,

Harold Johnson

L to R: Perreault, Paulson, Rockey, Johnson, and Riggins

negative or positive, with an employee. You catch the person where they are, and you give them hell. Not only are you creating barriers to the communications between you and them, you have established other negative forces, including, "How can I make my peers respect me for excellence when they have heard the boss chew me out about something else?"

I think it is kind of important to realize that few supervisors have ever been groomed for the job of supervision to the point that they test the limit of their authority to direct or control the activities of the subordinate. They grow into that position quite as they have in the other, learning a skill. By the time you learn it, you've either been promoted above it or you are locked into that with the preset of the work group believing, "Well, that's the way Joe is." Nobody would ever believe that Joe has the capacity to change. In many instances, especially in the public sector, the line supervisor has no involvement in the selection of personnel. "We have somebody that's coming in Tuesday and they're going to work with you." Not only that: they are going to be working at a given task and the supervisor doesn't have much authority to say, "Well, no I don't want to do that. I want to shift this other person to that role and I want to start someone else in a different one." I think if we speak to the deficiencies, though, of communication skills of supervisors and communication skills in dealing with subordinate personnel, it is not, altogether, a lack of grooming. In many instances, the selecting process—"Who got to supervision?"—was not based on the refinement of social skills, which includes communication skills. Supervisors don't get much assistance from management. Normally they learn how to communicate more effectively in a work environment. If they go to school or get it from somewhere else, what you're taught somewhere else rarely really applies in the work place. The rules change, and if you then begin to outshine the management above the line-level supervisor you are put to task immediately: "What do you think you're doing here. You're trying to change the whole world." To that point, I think the adaptation of supervisors to management is greater than adaptation to the needs of the employee.

The infusion of new people, new types of people of varied social, economic, political, religious, racial groupings, into a work force has compounded that delicate balance of "How effectively can a supervisor communicate?" Put those changes with the advent of the liberation of women and militant behavior brought on by social change, revolution etc., and the supervisor has a not too enviable position of trying to communicate with all the new forces put on him. Add human relation in management, with its emphasis on togetherness, and you have almost a paradoxical impasse. How can a supervisor meet all these demands? How can he meet any sort of production requirements?

I put those things together with the language problems. To mention some, I'll talk about the cultures that come out of the ghetto—the hardcore unemployment-type people that are being put into the labor force through various funding programs of the state and federal governments. The Mexican-American who rarely speaks anything other than Spanish in his home and in his community is now in the work place. You have to learn to understand what they are saying. The youth out of the black community, the dialect of the people, the jargon of the street, the permissiveness of the school systems, some of whom are reported to have skills and don't really have them. The infusion of today's social changes compounds supervisory communication skills disproportionate to the remuneration of the supervisor for the job he's got to do. I think that more time should be put or placed and more resources should be expended on development of skills of communication in various social or cultural groupings that are known to be included in the work force, prior to the appointment of the supervisor or at least that he should not be evaluated without consideration for those stresses that may occur.

And let's take as an example a clerical pool, you've got young employees, just out of high school, culturally deprived and oriented to what they perceive is resistance to the institution. You've got a supervisor that has to respond to management's identification with the institution. You've got another group of, let's say, the women in that same setting who resent the young ones who are now forced on them and are getting the relatively same pay they've been getting for forty years experience in the field. A lot of unrest in the work place, noise—the desire of some people to get radios going and various other distractors. At the same time the supervisor is trying to say, "Let me tell you you're not doing it right."

I have in the past four years presented counseling skills to various supervisors, and I have talked with people who have been supervisors for twenty years, fifteen years, five years, and this is their first opportunity to have a formal presentation on how to go about counseling: How do you work up a performance evaluation? How do you work the hardcore? I have a group working for me, and most of the time they use the vernacular that is meaningful to them, and I'm frustrated because I don't know what they're saying. How do you deal with that? You must stop and listen and you must listen to everything and understand them, even before they will care to understand you.

Management is frequently too busy to take time to tell supervisors what kind of problems management is having. I can't really put all the blame on management. They do have the problem of time and stress. At the same time, that goes down to the line level worker that the supervisor doesn't have time to listen to. My experience is that if you can teach people to listen with all their senses and not just their ears, they improve in their skills to communicate. Supervisors must only be in the job of supervising and not performing the task of productive activity. They must be pulled out of the work force and given a chance to learn who the people are, get close enough to them that they identify with them and function effectively.

Rockey: So often supervisors counsel employees when

either or both might be upset or in a crisis, defensive, or angry.

Perreault: Even though I was personally friendly with the president of a company where I was employed, at work we had an increasingly sharp edge between us, and finally we had a real old-fashioned blowout. It was the type of encounter in which you might well find yourself unemployed. After it was over and we talked, he said to me, "I'm really glad we had this blowout because I've been in management twenty years, now, and the only time I have a good discussion with a man is after I've fired him." So the simple fact is under normal circumstances you won't tell the man what you think, he won't tell you what he thinks and so you go along growing apart. Finally, you fire him. When you fire him, he then levels with you about what was wrong with your management, and your company, and your whole life style, and you tell him all that you think. It's too bad that it doesn't happen in an earlier stage.

Rockey: How can we change that?

Perreault: Well, he was proposing, in this particular case, talking of high levels of management within the company, there should be more person-to-person time. He said, "You know, you go on a weekend fishing together or off to a local resort where, in fact, you spend the weekend swimming and resting and visiting. Essentially, you have the occasion to talk back and forth, and some of these conflict things spill over." That's not possible across the board at all upper levels, but that was one of his thoughts.

Rockey: At least the more that happens, even if it can't be ideal, the more that that happens, more bridges are going to be built.

Johnson: One of the problems that happens with that, Ed, supervisors are not comfortable or confident or have never expressed to them the amount of authority to do anything about what seems to be going wrong. So they tend to defer anything until it comes to a head. The constant feedback is not there.

Rockey: So clear delegation of authority as well as responsibility, accountability, would open communication lines, and then the person would feel more confident to speak out in his or her area of authority.

Riggins: I had an experience many years ago, where I inherited a mess. In essence, it was a group of telephone operators who had been around for many, many years, and there were actually two or three of them that hadn't said a word to each other for a two-year period. So my task was to straighten this thing out. Number one, we did give the supervisor and the chief operator the authority to fire anyone at any time if they warranted it. We pointed out that they very well might be wrong. But that wasn't going to help the person that was fired. They're gone. They would become ineffective if we did not back them to that point. Then we also went into the technique of all new hires, upon interview, making it perfectly clear to them that if you got at cross fires with one of your fellow employees, try and work it out with that person. If you cannot work it out with that person then go to the supervisor and let the supervisor bring both people together and work it out. Do not let it build, because little things, just little misunderstandings here and there, if they are not solved at that time, the next week you have another little misunderstanding, finally it pyramids up to the point where there is a big blowoff. This was a preventative measure. It seemed to have a fairly good effect.

Johnson: I had the occasion, Ed, working with groups in training settings (especially when you get to role playing or acting out how you communicate) having supervisors in the presence of other peer supervisors admit that "I am afraid of that person that I am responsible for. I just don't feel comfortable addressing them in negative terms. Subsequently, things drift to the point where when I'm ready to fight enough, then I'm not afraid. The adrenalin is there, and anger overcomes my fear."

Rockey: We talked a lot about some problems, negative aspects, and they are very real. But I'm wondering, when you think of supervisors, employees, managers, administrators, executives, anyone in the organization who you feel has really been excellent—someone who is tops as a communicator—what activities or qualities do you associate with the people that you feel have been very successful organization communicators?

Paulson: Flexibility. Open mindedness.

Perreault: I would like to think that the people I admire in administration and the people that I would like to emulate are those who keep their communications on a low-key basis, day to day, so that they know the names of the people around them because they make a point to know the names. When they pass down the hall and they pass one of their associates, a member of the team, they address them by name. They are never too busy to take a minute and speak to the person, to express an interest. You've heard that there's an illness or that there is a change in location coming, or it is just simply that you haven't seen them in a long time. I think when you keep to your lines of communication that way, people feel that they are going to get a fair break from you. If they feel they have an avenue in which they can get a fair hearing, then they don't rile so much at the fact that their immediate supervisor is giving them a hard time. I have several cases of that at the present time where associates in our sister company here have not been getting the break that they feel that they should get, and they don't hesitate to drop in to talk small-talk. They will drop their message and I will go back into their system, and usually I find there is a misunderstanding as to what's going on and we smooth it out. They feel that freedom of communication.

Rockey: I think this is the answer to the problem we raised before, communicating only when it's a highly-charged negative kind of situation—being accessible, developing mutual trust, and having frequent low-key communications on a daily or weekly basis informally.

Johnson: There are several things about the success of the excellence of supervisory management skills in communication. I have to address myself to the leadership/followership. To have a position of leadership you have to have people willing to follow you. In order to realize that you have to satisfy the needs of people. When I consider that, I look at openness, honesty, fairness, flexibility, balance, trust, memory. How much do you remember about what my problem was three weeks ago? "You told me you'd get back to me and you never did. I have no confidence in you, that you ever really are listening."

Cordiality and sincerity of concern for the individual. I'm not saying you have to be overly friendly, if it isn't your nature. The effective communicating supervisor somehow instills confidence in his people. To instill that you have to delegate it. You have got to turn it loose and expect them to handle it. We live up to what's expected of us; even when it's beyond our capacity. Memory serves me again, back to 1962 and 1963, I worked for the finest boss or supervisor I ever had. His approach was, "I know you can handle it and if you need anything you'll come to me." I worked so hard for the man that I collapsed from fatigue and it put me in the hospital. He would never interfere, even when it was going badly: "Well, whatever you think. I have confidence in your judgment, and if I didn't I wouldn't have hired you."

Rockey: I think I hear you all saying: "The people who are really successful in communicating as managers aren't necessarily using some sophisticated techniques or modern methods, but they have certain personal qualities."

Perreault: Humanness.

Rockey: Being human, being there when needed. Mutual respect; friendliness; open mindedness. Keeping the ego trip out of it. Just sort of, on a day-to-day basis, keeping in touch in a really direct and sincerely involved way.

Riggins: You can probably go back to that one word again: Honesty. Be yourself.

Rockey: How do you react to this statement: "Good credibility means good communication."

Perreault: Generally speaking, an honest straightforward answer is a short answer. When you are communicating profusely, maybe overcommunicating, it's very often a matter of obfuscating of some kind. You're giving the person a lot of words and a lot of feeling that he is being communicated with but, in fact, what you are doing is avoiding the issues. A company which is putting out press releases every day, every hour on the hour, telling how great it is doing is, in fact, generally building a lack of credibility, not building credibility.

Johnson: I had a meeting in my office, oh it's been two years ago, in which I called some subordinate employees in to discuss what we were going to do with the system. About twenty minutes into the meeting my mind became saturated with another priority problem and I admitted the distraction: "I'd like to put you off for awhile. I can't deal with what we're dealing with now. My mind is on something else, and I'll get back to you." I dismissed the meeting. The next morning I called them in, and we spent quite a lot of time. The response and feedback came that morning: "You really weren't responding accurately with our input. It was a refreshing thing to have you admit the truth. Your mind wasn't on what you called the meeting for."

Rockey: That's a good point. When you *are* listening they would be thinking, "Well if he's really not listening, he's going to tell us. So he's probably listening."

Johnson: My credibility went up at the time.

Rockey: When does the informal communication network, whether it be the grapevine or gossip or whatever it might be, when does the informal communication network become more significant than the formal one? Is this good or bad or indifferent? What could or should be done about it?

Johnson: I guess the informal communication network is a subsystem, a backup system, to the major system. The most rapid communication goes through the grapevine, and it comes into play whenever employees feel that they're getting inadequate information or that something has been done unfairly. It may be totally fair, but if they don't perceive it as such, it's unfair.

   When I look at the grapevine I constantly look at it in the sense that grapevines are productive communication channels. They're free. They really don't cost you anything. They allow a catharsis to keep you from having to deal with problems. At the same time, I say that grapevines have to be pruned. I'll call a meeting and tell people: "I understand that this is a rumor; this is how I interpret it, and this is what you can believe in." You can put a brief stop to a vine or you can retrain it or train it back in the opposite direction, so that you have a bush rather than a sprawling vine.

Paulson: I like to separate the grapevine from the informal organization, and I do that primarily because I feel the grapevine is a negative word and it is associated with rumor. I deal with the informal organization in a positive sense. I believe it will rise spontaneously wherever you have people. I believe that it is a very effective organization. I believe in nurturing it and caring for it. I would say for a general manager, it would not be a good thing to recognize it openly, but to deal with it very quietly and use it. I think your most productive work comes from the informal organization. That's where you find upward and downward and horizontal communication at its best. I think you are eliminating a lot of disciplinary problems within that organization if you are aware of the informal organization. You reduce the amount of competition. The informal organization is a unit. It is a working unit and those people in that particular unit discipline their own ranks very well. There are, sort of, unspoken rules that accompany it. You don't take credit for a single idea. No individual ever does that. They work on the total project. I just want to make a distinction between the grapevine and the informal organization.

Rockey: One last question on this topic. If you were going to design a training program in effective communication for first-line supervisors, what would be the most urgent items to cover in a course that would include effective communication for supervisors?

Johnson: My experiences in the area of developing and doing programs has been, I guess, a growth experience not by any great wisdom, is to create an atmosphere in a training environment where people can experiment with what you know them to be deficient in. In truth, we learn by doing. You really never know how to measure your effectiveness until someone else is feeding back to you, "That was good or it wasn't good and this is what you did wrong."

How to structure a setting in which they are dealing with an employee, in which they are forced to confront the employee with what is unpleasant. How to allow the time for and to encourage ventilation on the part of the employee and on their own part to the proportion that's appropriate.

Paulson: We tailor communication programs to the organizational needs or the needs of supervisors, and my emphasis has been on the development of all human senses to better listening, which enhances and forces better organization and better communication and better human relations. That's the tack that I normally take. We do a lot of role playing and real life situational things. We may pick knotty kinds of problems which have occurred over the years and deal specifically with those.

Johnson: One additional thing on that. Once you've sat in the capacity of an authority on the development of a skill, you don't abandon the people as they go back and try their new skills. You remain accessible to them to insure that, "Okay, you tried this, and this is the reaction you got. I'd suggest you try the other thing." But you're not in the setting where they are influenced by your supposed excellence. They go back and try it on their own and modify it. You can even suggest to them, "Wait three or four days before you approach it again. Don't wait longer than a week." You can engineer, in absentia, much better than if you're on the spot trying to reactivate. Communicate to an individual or a group you're working with on the developing of their skills that, "I'm accessible to help you."

four

Planning for
Communication

OBJECTIVES

Readers should be able to effectively:

  set communication goals
  analyze audiences
  adapt to audiences
  find information
  organize materials
  put words together
  plan feedback and follow up

In the construction industry, regardless of the type of building involved, certain principles and practices apply uniformly.
No matter what type of structure you plan to erect, you
must go through some basic preliminary steps. So it is in
communication: some ideas and techniques apply to virtually all written and oral forms. In this chapter we will
discuss these common ideas and techniques; in the following chapter we will consider specific media.

ESTABLISH THE OBJECTIVE

Clarify for yourself the aim of the communication. If possible, write it in a single sentence. No part of the communication process carries more weight than this one. Exactly
what do you want the reader(s) or listener(s) to understand,
accept, or do? Most organizational messages fall into one of
the three following categories.

The Informative Message

The key goal of the informative message is to share information. The writer or speaker does not seek to change anyone's opinion; rather, the communicator merely wants to educate people.

For example, someone in the personnel division of an organization must inform employees of certain benefits. This information might come to employees through a brochure, a letter, an orientation session, or by some other medium. But the individual responsible must have a goal statement to work with, written or unwritten, spoken or unspoken. In this case, it could read, "All the employees of our company will understand the new benefits which have been added to our group hospitalization insurance."

Two additional examples of informative goal statements follow: "At the end of our interview, the two newly promoted supervisors will know where and when the three different weekly reports should be submitted." "By reading this brochure, customers who have purchased our Model M machine will know how to install the new adapter."

The Convincing Message

The convincing type of communication goes beyond informing and seeks to secure or reinforce acceptance. Letters, pamphlets, or speeches focusing on morale, public relations, or a defense of organizational policy often fall in this category. Sample goal statements for this type of communication follow: "The government agency and community groups reading this report will have assurance that our organization cooperates with environmental protection standards." "This pay envelope insert will help employees to see the necessity and fairness of our new absenteeism policy." Obviously, such goal statements do not appear in messages literally; rather, they serve as a focus and guide for the writer or speaker.

The Action Message

Some messages go beyond information and belief (though they may include these two goals) and seek to persuade listeners or readers to act. Sales presentations fall into this category. After the prospective client understands the nature of the product and comes to believe in the advantages of owning it, the sales transaction itself must occur. Many internal presentations involve seeking approval for changes or for expenditures within the organization.

Some action message goal statements follow: "The executive committee should approve the transfer of our legal staff to a consolidated division in St. Louis." "The project director will allow me to hire two more assistants when we actually start work on Project Q."

ANALYZE THE AUDIENCE

Whether you are sharing information, securing acceptance, or seeking action, you must deal with receivers, the audience who will read or hear your message. By definition, effective messages tend to be audience-centered.

Identify the Audience

Who will receive the communication? Will the readers or listeners be experts on the subject or will they know very

little about it? How well do I know the audience? What are
their loyalties? Has the audience ever expressed approval or
disapproval of ideas similar to the one I will be communicating? What interest does the audience have in this topic? How
much time will the audience have to give to this communication? Am I communicating with superiors, subordinates, or
both? What method of communication does the audience
prefer?

The questions above merely hint at the vast possibilities
for audience analysis. Naturally, you will have more time,
interest, and resources for studying some audiences than you
will for others. In writing a letter of complaint to a salesman,
you might do virtually no audience analysis. On the other
hand, if you were trying to close a million-dollar deal, you
might do quite a bit of research on the prospect.

Adapt to the Audience

Obviously, communicators do audience analysis for a
reason—so that the receivers will understand, believe, or act
upon the message. In order for audience analysis to become
productive we must present ideas in a manner acceptable to
and easily grasped by the audience.

Audience adaptation involves adjusting the substance
and style of the communication to fit the education, attitudes, interest, convenience, and general background of the
readers or listeners. Consider the following questions: What
words and concepts will the audience understand most readily? How much evidence will the audience require? Will the
choice of materials sustain interest? In what ways have I
taken audience viewpoints and commitments into consideration?

RESEARCH THE SUBJECT

Appropriate research varies widely: in writing some memos or letters, your memory alone may suffice; on the other hand, a vital organizational report may call for weeks or months of research. Some typical methods follow.

Questionnaires

This approach offers an opportunity to gather information quickly and inexpensively (compared with interviewing the same subjects one by one), even though the respondents may be widely scattered. This checklist will help make questionnaires effective:

1. Use specific, factual questions.
2. Include a set of brief, clear instructions.
3. Have the questions in logical order.
4. Limit each question to one topic or response.
5. Word the question in such a way that the likelihood of a prejudiced response is minimized.
6. Design the questionnaire so that the respondent can complete it in a short time.
7. Guarantee anonymity, when appropriate.
8. Include a stamped, self-addressed envelope.
9. Request the response by a particular date.

Here is an example of "how not to":

Have you used our new product and do you like it?

Following our guidelines above, we would reword this to read something like this:

How often have you used Brand Q?   never_____ once_____

twice_____ three times or more_____ .

How do you rate it? excellent_____ good_____ fair_____ poor_____.

Vague, long-winded, confusing, and inconvenient questionnaires will receive very few responses, if any. Usually a questionnaire is filled in and returned as a courtesy; make everything as brief, convenient, and clear as possible.

Interviews

You will find further information about interviewing in the last chapter of this text. Interviews offer access to information which cannot be gathered in any other way. In a face-to-face situation direct feedback occurs, with many nonverbal cues, and the immediacy of the situation often stimulates questions and observations which might not surface otherwise.

Library Sources

By consulting a reference librarian most novice researchers discover resources they never dreamed existed. Some metropolitan and university libraries have special business reference librarians, and many corporations and nonprofit organizations maintain special libraries.

You may discover that an index exists for periodicals in the field you are researching. Such an index can save you many hours of digging. The index will cover several periodicals in a given field, though the *Reader's Guide to Periodical Literature* indexes materials from popular general magazines. But the *Business Periodicals Index* lists articles from business-related magazines only.

You may want to consult a book on available resources,

such as *Sources of Business Information* by E. T. Coman.
You may also consult various government publications and
business directories. This communication text cannot catalog
all such materials, but the hints given should point you in a
resourceful direction.

Observations and Experiments

Sometimes reports contain documented observations (of
working conditions or employee performance, for example).
Quite often presentations are supported by experiments the
writer or speaker has conducted. Such experiments do not
necessarily involve elaborate laboratory procedures. Perhaps
an employee secured an "OK from the boss" and then pro-
ceeded to try some new operation or production technique.
Such innovations do not always require much more personnel
or material, but, if successful, they may prove to be very
strong supports for recommended changes.

ORGANIZE THE MATERIALS MEANINGFULLY

The framework of a building, the plot of a novel, and the
skeleton in your body all suggest that some sort of sub-
structure is usually needed to hold things together and to
help them make sense. Organizational communications, too,
need meaningful structure. Such a framework will help both
writers and speakers achieve clarity, unity, logic, and completeness. Singly or in combination, ten standard structural
patterns can help us as we attempt to arrange data meaningfully.

Time Order

This approach becomes helpful when we move backwards or forwards in a chronological sense. You may want to use this type of structure when discussing expenses or sales during certain months, quarters, or years. Most statements about profits and losses use a time frame.

Space Order

Reports often combine time order and space order, the latter referring to particular places. Such reports focus on what happened in certain locations over a period of time. International organizations may refer to continents or nations. Nationwide groups may use such terms as north and south, eastern and western divisions, or mention various states of the country. Other types of spatial terms are used such as county, city, district, precinct, and so on. Some messages refer to locations based on other types of arrangements, where no specific boundaries pertain such as urban and rural.

Cause-Effect

This type of development serves us well when we deal with "why" something happened. The order may be effect to cause or cause to effect, but in either case, a direct, causal relationship is involved. Accident reports usually trace causes, and reports on innovative programs usually stress effects.

Problem Solution

Recommendations for future action often embody this type of structure because so many suggestions center on

solving problems. The establishment of need usually pre-
cedes the offering of a solution. A standard problem solution pattern involves these steps: What is the problem? What
caused it? What are the trends in the problem? By what standards should we evaluate possible solutions? What are the
recommended solutions? Which solution(s) best meet the
standards? How will we put the best solution(s) into effect?

Increasing Difficulty

This framework involves going from the simple to the
complex or from the familiar to the unfamiliar. Such a pattern is especially useful when readers or listeners do not have
expertise in the subject under consideration. Quite often
specialists or professionals fail to observe this order when
speaking to laymen or nonprofessionals and confusion results.

Established Category

This approach to structuring a communication implies
that some basic frameworks are widely understood and that
the subject under consideration falls into one such framework. Some well-known examples of established categories
follow: executive, legislative, and judicial; private and public
sectors; federal, state, and local; profit or nonprofit; domestic
and foreign; and line and staff. We are all familiar with various ways to categorize people (by age, sex, nationality, and
so on).

Inductive or Deductive

Inductive reasoning involves the development of an idea
in such a way that we move from the specific to the general.

The communicator begins by referring to particular details and moves toward a general conclusion. On the other hand, the deductive order moves from a general statement to the supporting particulars.

Comparison or Contrast

When we trace differences or similarities the issues or items which are placed side by side come into sharper focus than if they remain isolated. This approach naturally accompanies the description of advantages or disadvantages connected with respective proposals.

Process Order

This arrangement is especially useful when explaining the steps involved in any activity. Often a flow chart accompanies such an explanation. If you were attempting to describe the stages in the manufacture of a product, the process order would be appropriate.

Pro and Con Order

This involves presenting the argument for and against a given proposal. It can be used when a writer or speaker feels that it is necessary to present all sides of a problem, without taking sides, and leaving it to the audience to make a decision.

DEVELOP AN APPROPRIATE STYLE

The way we put words together says a great deal about us— about our sense of logic, taste, accuracy, and clarity. The way we write and speak also says quite a bit about our organization, because people tend to view us as representatives of our organization. Though manuals of style must be consulted for a more comprehensive treatment, the following suggestions will serve as a helpful checklist.

Use Concrete Words

Abstract terms tend to be vague or ambiguous. Concrete words tend to be clear and specific; often they appeal to our senses—seeing, hearing, touching, tasting, smelling. In which column below do you find sharper detail?

He was generous to me.	He gave me a gift.	He gave me a gold watch.
Inclement weather set in.	It snowed.	Thirteen inches of snow fell in eight hours.
Productivity is down	We're producing less than we did last month.	With the same work force, we produced nine percent less than last month.

Most of us have to discipline ourselves to rewrite, to consult a dictionary or thesaurus, or to think of a more tangible way to express an idea. But it's worth the effort. Specify. Itemize. Give details or examples. Define. Illustrate.

Keep Sentences Short

This does not mean that brevity, of itself, produces clarity. For instance, which of the two following sentences is more clear, the one with three words or the one with eight? "Make a real effort to avoid being obscure." "Assiduously eschew obfuscation." But shorter sentences generally are more readable than longer sentences, other things being equal.

Lengthy sentences are usually more difficult to follow than shorter ones, and they are more likely to result in confusion or complexity. Some writers recommend an average sentence length of sixteen to eighteen words for the typical adult reader, but to prove to yourself that sentences may have over twice that many words with little loss in clarity, count the number of words in the sentence you are now reading.

Actually, no suggestion in this checklist, of itself, guarantees anything; however, in most cases shorter sentences with more concrete words will prove more readable than longer sentences with abstract words.

Vary Sentence Types and Structures

Declarative sentences make assertions, and *interrogative* sentences ask questions. "His report seems sound to me. Don't you agree?"

Imperative sentences give commands, and *exclamatory* sentences, well, . . . they exclaim. "Call the staff together immediately. Fantastic!"

In addition to having these four types of sentences at our disposal, we also have four basic sentence structures. This *simple* sentence has one independent clause. This *compound* sentence has two independent clauses separated by a conjunction, but it could contain three or more independent clauses. Continuing with the possibilities, this *complex* sentence has both an independent clause and a dependent clause. ("Continuing with the possibilities" is a dependent clause, since it does not make complete sense by itself and depends upon the independent clause following it to complete the meaning.) Completing our list, this *compound-*

complex sentence opens with a dependent clause, but it has at least two independent clauses, and we could add three or more.

. In any event, using the same basic sentence patterns over and over leads to monotony. For example, a series of simple declarative sentences usually seems childish and dull. But the same ideas in those sentences, put in a variety of sentence types and structures, can be expressed in a more compelling and interesting way.

Maintain Unity

Generally, try to build each paragraph around one idea or topic. Often writers can check on this principle by looking for an expressed or implied topic sentence around which the paragraph is built. If you discover two or more topic sentences in a paragraph, you should rewrite.

Use Active Verbs

What differences do you notice among the following pairs of sentences?

Passive	*Active*
As the committee meeting was opened, the financial crisis was discussed by the chairman.	As the committee meeting opened, the chairman discussed the financial crisis.
The plans were approved by the manager, and then they were mailed to Lima by a secretary.	The manager approved the plans, and a secretary mailed them to Lima.
His application for transfer is being submitted because his health is becoming worse in his present job.	He has applied for a transfer because his present job endangers his health.

Probably you perceive the active sentences as more forceful, and more direct. This does not mean that you should never use the passive voice; sometimes you will deliberately emphasize words other than active verbs. ("It must be submitted by *him*, and by no one else.") But strive to use active forms more often, and you will achieve a stronger and more straightforward effect.

Avoid Wordiness

Do the following sentences say the same thing?

Your check in the amount of $5,000.00 has been received.	Your $5,000.00 check arrived.

The words "in the amount of" merely pad the sentence. Many business letters and memos contain overused, wordy expressions. Note the following comparisons:

May I call your attention to the fact that the bill herewith enclosed was not paid promptly by the date payment was due?	Please note that this bill was not paid by the due date.
Owing to the fact that your organization has not regularly been delivering the goods in question in a prompt manner, we are forced to take this means to give you formal notice that in the future your services will no longer be required by our firm.	Because of so many late deliveries, we plan to use a different carrier.
In the event that you find yourself unable to supply us with desks which are of the secretarial type, with reference to our order of January 24, it should be noted that we require notice from you prior to February 21 on intent not to deliver.	If you cannot deliver the secretarial desks we ordered on January 24, please let us know by February 20.

In short, say it in as few words as possible.

Use Various Means of Emphasis

In any message certain points usually have more importance than others. How can you emphasize the more important points?

1. Space. Give a larger proportion of your communication to the most urgent concerns.
2. Repetition. Repeat priority items.
3. Position. In letters, speeches, reports, and so on, material brought up at the very beginning or the end or both receives a natural emphasis.
4. Mechanical means. In written communications or in visual aids accompanying oral presentations, underscoring, using color, capitalizing, "white space," and drawing arrows all give prominence to material.

Write and Speak Naturally

Admittedly, this suggestion sounds vague. What is "natural"? Probably your conversational language, when you are in a semiformal organizational setting, serves as a helpful guide. Would you hand your boss an envelope and say, "Herewith please find enclosed as per your request the file in question."? Of course not. You would probably say, "Here is the file you asked for." Fine! That is appropriate language for a letter.

Avoid the habit of writing speeches out word for word. Such speeches usually sound stuffy and unnatural. (You will find more information on this topic in the Oral Presentation section of Chapter Five.)

PLAN FOR FEEDBACK

So often we assume that because we have written or said something, we have "gotten the message across." This assumption causes innumerable communication problems, and we must build in feedback loops as we plan communications so that we can reduce such problems.

Feedback comes in many ways. We can observe reactions. We can use suggestion systems or questionnaires. We can enter into dialogue, with an opportunity for questions and answers. We can ask others to restate a message in their own words, and we can offer to restate their messages. In some appropriate way, we must build in an assurance system, so that we have confirmation that we understand each other.

FOLLOW UP

In many cases a one-time message does not get optimum results. Send out minutes of committee meetings and conferences, highlighting decisions and delegated responsibilities. Schedule progress reports after assigning tasks. Confirm important telephone calls, briefings, and interviews with memos. Constantly ask yourself, "Does this communication need reinforcement?"

CONCLUSION

This chapter has reviewed several vital questions which affect the planning of communications. Why am I sending this communication? To whom am I sending it? How should I adapt it for the receiver(s)? Where will I get the needed information? How should I organize the information? How should I word the message? How can I be sure that the message is understood as I intended? Does the message need reinforcement? Knowledgeable answers to these questions will go a long way toward making organizational communication more effective.

SKILL DEVELOPERS

1. Write four one-sentence goals for four different oral or written communication activities.
2. Write a three-page plan for an organizational report. Include such items as goal, audience, method of research, type of structure, expected outcome, format, special problems to overcome in researching or reporting, sources of evidence, and the significance of the report.
3. Rewrite for concreteness (obviously, you must invent details):
   a. She did good work.
   b. Unfortunately, various objects cluttered the work area.
   c. It was a successful conference.
4. Rewrite for variety:
   The reports arrived in my office on Thursday afternoon. They were a day late. One report was incomplete. Jones had written it. I called him immediately. He became defensive. He said he was overworked. He finally agreed to have the report ready by Monday. I had all the reports reviewed by my assistant on Wednesday. We sent them to headquarters on Friday. They were approved the next week.

5. Rewrite for brevity:

In the event that your check in the amount of $312.41 does not arrive in a prompt manner, we shall be forced to take steps along the lines of legal action. In view of the fact that we plan to pursue this matter to its resolution, you may wish to take appropriate action with reference to the aforementioned sum.

PANEL DISCUSSION

Riggins: I direct this into a line management-type situation and to my personal philosophy, and I think I use a little bit of this and a little bit of that and a little bit of something else from various theories. The important thing is to gain a personal insight into the individual you're trying to communicate with, if at all possible. On an individual basis, maybe communicating with an employee, try to understand that there may be personal problems. I think this would apply, too, if you're giving a presentation to a group of people. Try to ask yourself, "Is this a mixed group, say from the janitor to the vice president or is this a group of secretaries who are pretty much on the same level?" If you can gain that insight, I think you can better communicate with them. Adapt material to the background of the educational level, etc. You can come across a lot better that way. For instance, take the example of a drilling foreman in an oil patch. I don't know how many of you people have ever been in an oil patch. I'll tell you some of those fellows out there are rough characters.

Rockey: Aren't they called "roughnecks"?

Riggins: "Roughnecks." That's the name. In the telephone business they call them "grunts." It's a pretty rough crew. Like you say, if you use your 45¢ words on these people, you're not going to get your message across. By the same token, if you're going upstairs to talk to the executive V.P. about planning or budgeting or something like that, shift gears. So try to speak on the level of the person or group you're speaking to.

If you're writing or speaking to a group, explaining a function or an operation or something like that, it's my opinion that you direct it to the *lowest* level. I think its better to possibly have some people in the group say, "This guy thinks we're a bunch of dummies;" you still get your message across to the entire group.

Harold R. Riggins

Edward H. Rockey

Definitely, credibility must be established and maintained. Otherwise, we may as well be speaking to a stone wall. Another consideration is not to say in a thousand words which can be said in ten as long as the message gets across.

Johnson: You touched an interesting point that I would like to get your feeling about. When you move to the vernacular of the group, when do you determine when to start using common vernacular or four-letter words or whatever their jargon happens to be?

Riggins: I'm not dealing with the public, I am dealing with my own people in my company that I am familiar with, or pretty much familiar with. So it doesn't take very long to talk to someone—to say a few words—and get them to talk to you first, if you can. Ask a couple of leading questions. Then, at least it gives you a feel for that person.

Johnson: When you are making a formal presentation, never be late, so that you can mingle a little bit and find how they're talking, so that you can address yourself in their language. In your own work group or internal organization, don't put your mouth in gear until your ears have absorbed what it takes to make it work right.

Rockey: One thing that Hal mentioned as very significant in effective adaptation of communication in organization is gaining a personal insight of the individual, adjusting to the individual, and you said that one way you do this is by listening to the first few sentences. In order to do that we have to get feedback; you have to get the other person involved to know where they're at. I was wondering, in your experience, what methods of increasing the flow of feedback work best? Whether it's a presentation or a phone call or an interview or a committee meeting or discussion or training session, whatever communication situations we want to bring in, in your experience, what has worked best to increase the flow of feedback?

Riggins: In my particular field, as I said earlier, I started out drilling holes in concrete and went on into various stages, on into management, so establish the fact that "you've been there." You know what they're doing and why they're doing it, and it puts you in an advantageous position because you can direct questions to them and say something like, "I recall when I was doing that such and such happened." It puts the individual somewhat at ease: he thinks, "this guy has done the same thing I'm doing" and so forth and so now you've opened a path. He's free to talk because he says, "Okay, he knows what I'm saying because he's done it." I think that's the most effective way.

Paulson: You have to be conscious of developing feedback mechanisms. Where they come or how are they placed, I'm not sure. I think it's extremely important, but I'm not sure where they come in. How you do that is a matter of the planning and organization process, the development of definitive jobs, the understanding between subordinates and the boss or the leader whatever that situation might be. I think it creates accountability and establishes respect.

Riggins: I think any employee has to know what is expected of him and have it thoroughly understood. How do you communicate that to him? Here is one way. We have in our company a performance review, and we also have a job description which outlines duties and so forth. In this performance review thing you'll notice it says "Job Requirements." Describe the major responsibilities and goals of this job. Outline all of that, and then establish achievement measures, and then respond to the achievement measures over here on an appraisal basis. The way we work this is very simple, because we're given that much liberty to handle it ourselves. The way a lot of us do it we will fill out this part of the form as a manager and then we will hand a copy of it to the employee and say, "make your comments over here, and I'll make my comments over here, and then we'll get together and discuss it; these are not imbedded in concrete." Due to some misunderstanding or something like that then the results, the achievement, could have a different answer over here. But when you can actually put it down and discuss it item by item, now you are communicating and getting the idea across. I think that probably 90 percent of poor performance in any employee is the lack of understanding of what is expected of him.

Johnson: Performance review is supposedly used as a tool for communication when it really isn't. If you wait until then, there is no communication, nor will you ever create it by the document. The evidence that comes through in them should be used, and I say "should" by my own direction, as an indicator of the deficiency of the communication skills of the supervisor, for the management to use in addressing themselves to an employee understanding what they're supposed to do or what they're required to do. I have found damn few managers who can be concise in a statement of what they expect others to do. To refine the communication process, can you be precise in what you expect?

Perreault: I have a feeling when we give a man a formal review and we have a system for formal review, I try to make a statement that this man has a potential. He is suitable for operations at one or two or three levels above his present work and he should be given the opportunity to expand his knowledge to training courses. That's a generality. The next thing is that I try to tell the man, I consider that I have to put in writing to the man, "this is what's wrong with your operation. Are you too autocratic in your operation? You do not delegate responsibility. You fail to team yourself with the management, and therefore, the employee feels that in fact it's his proper role. You dress sloppily. You are a non-conformist in the environment where there is some need for conformity." I try to make it specific that the man might read and understand when it is in writing, and he's signed it off and, in fact, these are the areas where he's not really doing his job. If I fail to do that, almost invariably when you bring a man in to tell him that he's been demoted or put in the street or whatever the case may be, it always comes as a shock to him. I've never talked to a man who was being demoted or put out of an operation who isn't totally shocked and offended and surprised. I think that all of us waltz around the issue like it's distasteful to discuss with a man what's wrong with him, what he is doing wrong. I think you have to put it down in writing and make him understand that this is the way it is.

In aerospace we have a lot of expansion and a lot of contraction. In one Lockheed company where we went from 32,000 people to 9,500 in the engineering branch it was always typical the supervisor would say what a fine man this fellow was. What fine work he did. He would sign that paper every six months for fifteen years. Once a year he'd get a merit raise because of the job he was doing. Now we have to let a lot of people go and now the manager has to decide, "who do I retain." He'd bring the papers forward and look at the file saying, "We're going to give this man his notice," and the chief engineer would say, "What are you giving him notice about," Then he'd say, "Well you know he's always tardy," or "You can't depend on him." They go through all the reviews and he said, "Look, there is no way I'll give consideration to laying off a man on a performance basis until we've had two reviews, in writing, in that folder that says that a man isn't doing his job. Now, since you haven't given those reviews on this man I can't accept that. Go find a man whose work you have challenged." It made quite a difference in that department from then on.

Johnson: I've seen an instance where an individual had been given a very negative evaluation and the reviewer of the evaluation took a different tack on it, and I think very effectively. He said, "This is the evaluation you want me to sign as the reviewer." It was like, I'd say 80 percent negative. "I will sign it if that's what you want put through," he said, "But I'll tell you what I expect you to do as a result of it. The evidence is so preponderant that you are deficient in your supervisory skills that I am going to have to do one on you." Immediately thereafter the performance of both people improved. To the point of courage in managing, if you have allowed that person to flow through for a year with all these problems and have done nothing about it, you're deficient and the evidence you present me is that it's your own conviction, in a sense.

Rockey: Hal, does this appraisal form—review form—include communication as a skill?

Riggins: I'll read you one comment: "How does the employee need to improve in his present job? A need to improve his ability to communicate orally, in groups especially. Needs to improve his writing and reporting techniques."

Rockey: This is your comment?

Riggins: This is my comment and then this was reviewed with the employee. He said, "You're not telling me anything new. I've known that since the fourth grade." Then I said, "Why haven't you done something about it?"

Rockey: Does the appraisal review form specifically ask you to discuss the employee's communication skills?

Riggins: No. It doesn't come right out and ask that.

Perreault: I had an experience in my younger days. I had a man who worked for me who was of Dutch descent, raised in Holland, spoke four languages and was an historian by avocation. I travelled with him quite a bit, and as far as I was concerned he knew everything—brilliant, and I enjoyed being with him. One day talking of this particular man to my supervisor, I made some comment on him, and I said I don't know what his I.Q. is but I would guess it would be very high. The gentleman said, "I don't think it's a very high I.Q." So we called up the department where they had that information just for amusement to find out what was the man's I.Q. His basic mental ability, as we call it on our forms around here, was I guess 117 or 118. His language M.A. was up in the area of 160. We went into a discussion of this which I had never really thought of in that sense before. My associate said, "In the final analysis it really doesn't matter how much you know or how brilliant you are because that's buried in you. Nobody has the opportunity to weigh that unless you're a research scientist or something, someone who is working in a very finite field where he can exercise his brilliance in a vacuum. Principally, we measure people on what they communicate to us." So a man who has a moderate level of intelligence can communicate that readily to his associates and to the application of his job. It isn't only that he sounds better and makes a better impression and does a better job: it's that he actually performs better. What you know that is buried inside your head or your body or your heart but which does not have a day-to-day interest and talent to communicate, doesn't really mean very much. Unless you end up operating in a vacuum, and I guess I believe that more and more, it's wonderful to have a man of tremendous depth, but if he can't communicate it at any level, who does it benefit?

Johnson: I think that touches another interesting point. Effective communication and the utilization of whatever level of intelligence a person has is much more dependent, and it sort of gets back to something else: Can you relate to the individual, and can you somehow identify with what you are there communicating in some sort of a common analogy? What do we identify with?

five

Using
Specific Media

OBJECTIVES

By applying the principles and practices of this chapter, readers should improve effectiveness in:

  leading meetings
  conducting interviews
  giving oral presentations
  writing letters and reports

During a typical week, most managers or administrators send letters and memos, make phone calls, interview, and conduct meetings. This chapter outlines key considerations for half a dozen organizational media. As you read this chapter please keep three points in mind. First, you can find entire volumes on such distinct topics as interviewing, writing letters, conducting meetings, and making presentations.

Secondly, the suggestions in the preceding chapter, "Planning for Communication," apply to the media in this chapter. Finally, the choice of a medium has become more complex in the age of McLuhan, who has helped us to see that each medium is a message in itself: the written word cannot sigh, laugh or groan, but the telephone voice can; the telephone voice cannot wince, nod, shake hands, raise eyebrows, or give eye contact, but such events can occur in a face-to-face interview.

CONDUCTING MEETINGS

Almost every organization has staff meetings, committees, and conferences. Unfortunately, many employees enter such sessions with the attitude, "Well, here we go, another time-waster" or "Ho hum, another dull meeting." What can we do to make meetings more productive and encourage more participation?

Before the Meeting

The success of a meeting starts before the meeting begins. Following several vital steps beforehand will help guarantee a productive session. (1) Send an early notice to all participants including the starting and closing time, the location, the tentative agenda, and the goal(s) of the meeting. This will allow people to clear their calendars and to come prepared. (2) Request that additional agenda items be sent to you before the meeting. This will encourage participation and will help you prepare for the meeting. (3) If a regularly scheduled meeting is not needed, *cancel it.* If you have no agenda, why meet? (4) Anticipate and prevent distractions: secure all necessary materials in advance, meet in a traffic-free area, have telephones covered, and so on.

If you have control over the size and composition of the group, research has indicated that five to seven members make an ideal number. Larger groups become unwieldy, and smaller groups often get into awkward power struggles. Of course, organizational realities or the need for resource people may create committees outside of the "ideal" range.

Write out a tentative outline of the meeting, taking your goals into consideration. Will you be gathering information, giving information, solving problems, making decisions, brainstorming, or gaining cooperation? The dynamics of the group will create the actual structure of the meeting, but it helps to come in with a general idea of the desired progress of the session.

Procedures During the Meeting

After brief social amenities (saying hello, getting coffee, and so on), have a clear point of beginning for the session. This opening need not be the hackneyed "come to order" approach. You may open pointedly by moving to a flip chart or chalkboard and restating the purpose of the meeting or reviewing the agenda.

With the agenda before them, the group should submit additional agenda items and then proceed to rank the agenda items. When the most urgent concerns have been identified, the order of topics to be considered and the amount of time to be spent on each should be agreed upon.

Begin the discussion of each topic by gathering as much objective data as possible. Of course, we can quibble about the term "objective" for a few centuries, and we can argue that our feelings are facts—"it's a *fact* that I *feel* irritated right now!" But if we look at objective and subjective material on a continuum, tend to open discussions with data from the objective end.

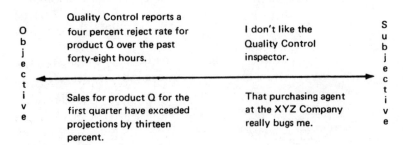

Eventually, you must deal with values, opinions, feelings, and relationships. Personal judgments must be considered. That's one basic reason for management meetings; otherwise, we could feed hard data to computers and have decisions made for us. But we tend to reach agreement more readily regarding objective data than we do regarding subjective data. If we begin discussions with the "hard facts," we may build some consensus before we move on to opinionated concerns.

Involve people effectively. If the group has been chosen wisely, several types of human resources will be present in the group, with some individuals possessing several vital qualities:

1. Task orientation; people who get the job done.
2. Knowledgeable individuals.
3. Idea people; creative minds.
4. Compromisers; adaptable individuals.
5. Participative members.
6. Social leaders.
7. Communicators who know the larger organization.

Identify each issue carefully. Be sure that each individual understands the problem, and that everyone focuses on it. Maintaining relevance often becomes a challenge to a committee leader. One way to handle significant but irrelevant material is to write any new topic down at the bottom of the agenda, agreeing to consider it in due course, and then move back to the issue under consideration.

Often both pertinence and progress can be achieved through the effective use of questions. Overhead questions are worded so that anyone can answer them; targeted questions are directed toward a given individual. Closed-ended questions call for the type of answer implicit in the question: "How many new employees did we hire last month?" Open-ended questions allow for a wide range of responses: "How can we reduce turnover?" Thus, "Leslie, do you know whether or not this practice fulfills the federal regulation?" serves as an example of a closed-ended targeted question, and "Does anyone have some suggestions for improving the purchasing procedures?" exemplifies the open-ended overhead type.

A tactful chairperson can help prevent one of the most common problems of committees—the hidden agenda. Sometimes participants (or, too often, nonparticipants) have issues they want to bring into the discussion or put on the agenda, but they do not. While worrying about these hidden agendas, they fail to concentrate on the issues before the group. The alert observer of nonverbal cues, the active listener, the individual who welcomes dissenting viewpoints will create a climate in which hidden agendas are not likely to surface.

The Outcome of the Meeting

One of the signs that meetings fall short of effectiveness goes something like this: "I thought we decided that last month" or "Who was supposed to take care of that?" These symptoms of committee illness can be helped by the following procedures:

1. Identify group decisions clearly.
2. Send concise minutes to all participants (not a blow-by-blow account of the meeting; just the decisions, recommendations, and assignments).
3. Delegate responsibility for each decision.
4. Require progress reports on follow-through.
5. Inform all participants of progress and results.

INTERVIEWING

Most managers spend more time in face-to-face sessions with

one or two individuals than they do with larger groups. Interviews serve several purposes:

1. Hiring people.
2. Explaining policies or changes.
3. Developing employees.
4. Handling grievances.
5. Reviewing performance.
6. Counseling.
7. Disciplining.
8. Assigning responsibility.
9. Getting progress reports.
10. Terminating.
11. Brainstorming.

Specialized manuals offer particular guidelines for closely defined types of interviews, but this volume will deal only with general principles which apply to all kinds of interviews. Naturally, the material in the chapter "Management Style and Communication" applies to the interviewing task.

Preparing for the Interview

Occasionally unplanned, spontaneous interviews occur; however, when you have time and opportunity, several preliminary steps give greater assurance of success in interviewing:

1. Identify the specific purpose(s) of each interview. When the employee leaves the interview, what should have been decided, solved, or understood?
2. Inform the other party ahead of time about the nature of the interview, and request any advance preparation necessary. You will probably create anxiety

if you give no explanation beforehand. An employee of a public school in Texas heard she was wanted in a school official's office, and she assumed that she was "on the carpet for being too outspoken;" actually, she discovered that a school was being named after her because of her devoted service.

3. Do as much advance research as you can so that the interview will move productively and not be interrupted by searches for data.

4. Although you will certainly adapt the flow of the interview according to realities which you cannot always anticipate, have a tentative outline ready.

5. Write out specific questions which will help you fulfill your goals for the interview.

6. Do a preliminary exploration of possible outcomes and the effects of those outcomes.

7. Learn as much about the interviewee as possible.

8. Decide whether you want a highly structured interview or a free-flowing approach.

9. If appropriate, inform the other party of the time allotted for the interview, and arrange for a graceful close (for example, a secretary might call you to remind you that "your next appointment is in five minutes.") Of course, certain emotionally-charged interviews or emergency situations may have to preempt later appointments.

Conducting the Interview

The interview begins when the other individual enters. Do you shake hands or not? Do you close the door? Do you "hold all calls"? Do you offer refreshments? Where do you sit? I exercised my memory to try to recall how I used my office during my work in an administrative role, and I could think of only one instance when I seated someone with my desk between us: it was a disciplinary interview. In all other cases, we sat in "equal" chairs around a small round table.

Preview the session with the interviewee. Discuss the basic reason(s) for the meeting, and, if appropriate, the procedure and expected outcome. This could be done indirectly, in the form of a question; "Before I assign that project we talked about last week, do you have any questions we should discuss?"

Create a helpful climate in the interview situation. Is the interviewee anxious or confused? How can you help? Have you extended courtesy and respect? Above all, are you really listening? Have you tuned in to the other person's needs, attitudes, and expectations? That does not mean that you must fulfill such needs, accept such attitudes, or honor such expectations, but empathic listening involves understanding.

Encourage participation. We learn virtually nothing while we talk; if we want to learn more about the other person's problems or awareness, we must ask relevant questions and listen. Maintain the most helpful balance between control and spontaneity. Use open-ended questions when you have the time and opportunity to explore and listen; use specific, focused questions and comments when you must move in a more directed manner.

Close purposefully. The interviewee should know such things as: What has been decided? Who will carry out which responsibilities? What must be reported to whom by when? Must a follow-up interview be scheduled? Often it helps to put the outcome of the interview in writing, sending a copy to the interviewee.

GIVING ORAL PRESENTATIONS

An unscientific survey convinced me that, in schools which require a speech course for graduation, students postpone speech more than they put off any other course. "Stage fright" may be a major reason for dreading speech-making, but the oral business presentation is more informal than traditional speech-making, and virtually every manager must demonstrate the ability to stand up before a group of people and to present an idea coherently and believably.

Often management presentations appear in connection with committees or interviews: you may be asked to present a proposal to one person—probably your boss or your boss's boss; you may be asked to present your proposal to a decision-making group, who will then discuss it and make a decision one way or the other.

In connection with preparing oral presentations, you should review several points from the preceding chapter, "Planning for Communication": establishing the objective, identifying the audience, adapting to the audience, researching the subject, and organizing the material meaningfully. After reviewing the material in the preceding chapter, consider the following additional points:

Prepare for Audience Response

Most oral presentations receive immediate feedback, and you get this response while you are still in the actual presentation situation. Contrast this with a written report, which you complete some time before submitting it and which may not be discussed for several days.

Be ready for the emotional strain of possible refutation from the audience, most or all of whom may be above you in the organization. Audiences may challenge your sources,

your conclusions, or your reasoning. Avoid defensive responses, and yield gracefully to facts and to experience when
appropriate. When you know you're right, stand your ground
courteously and professionally: don't prove your point and
lose your proposal.

Try to foresee the effects of your proposal on various
audience concerns:

profit	organizational relationships
personnel	company image
morale	company policy
clients	established procedures
schedules	government regulations
competitors	labor unions

Be prepared to discuss impacts on such aspects.

Build an Effective Introduction and Conclusion

Unfortunately, studies reveal that audience attention
tends to be highest when you open and when you say, "in
conclusion" or "finally." The introduction should involve
the audience, suggest what will follow and move aptly into
the main body of the presentation.

Avoid lame openings, such as "Well, as you all already
know, I'm supposed to talk about our sales for this quarter,
and I only wish I'd had more time . . ." That's a loser from
the word "well."

One way to begin such a presentation involves the use
of a line graph such as this one. You could start by drawing
only the projected line (with the rest of the graph previously
prepared on a flip chart or chalkboard), and saying something
like, "You probably know that this was our projected sales
figure for the first quarter of this year. But what did we
actually achieve?" Then proceed to draw the actual sales

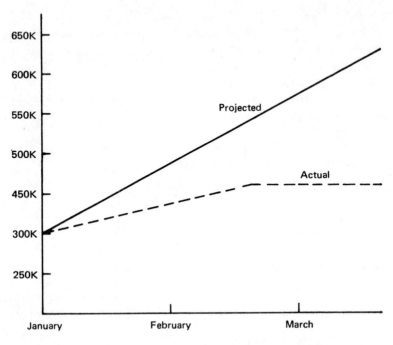

line. This approach uses some of the principles of attention: concreteness is involved in the use of a graph with numbers; expectancy appears in the opening question; relevance comes out in the relationship between the graph and the purpose of the meeting; and an ongoing or purposeful quality emerges in the inference that you are about to reveal something which is related to the preceding information and which helps complete it.

The conclusion of the presentation should either restate your key points, using a fresh approach, or emphasize your principal goal, or both. Avoid weak endings: don't ramble or apologize, "Well, er um, I guess that's all, and I wish I'd had more time to prepare ..."; don't introduce new concepts in the conclusion; avoid hackneyed phrases such as "May I state in conclusion."

Vary the Types of Material in the Presentation

Engineers may tend to use only technical data, sales people may tend to overuse personal experiences. As you gather your materials look for relevant variety.

1. Pertinent quotations, perhaps from leaders in your field or your organization.
2. Relevant statistical data.
3. Incidents from your own background or the experience of others.
4. Analogies or other types of verbal illustrations.
5. Physical illustrations.
6. Definitions.
7. Explanations.
8. Demonstrations.

In connection with the last point, nothing seems more believable than a demonstration, whether it is a complex piece of machinery or a simple act. Once I gave a series of training classes to some airline managers and they rehearsed presentations in the class. One of them, a food service manager, wanted to convince the airline to replace foil food containers with fiber ones. He brought to class some pastry packed in one of the fiber containers. As we bit into the sweet, moist bakery goods, we became instant believers.

Plan Visual Aids Carefully

Visual aids tend to make material graphic and vivid. Some concepts or relationships demand visualization; mere verbalization could not make the situation clear. For example, imagine trying to explain the workings of an internal combustion engine with no visual aids.

In planning to use visual aids, keep one distinction clear—
the difference between the type of visual aid and the medium
of presentation.

Visual Aids	Media of Presentation
pie charts	chalkboard
bar graphs	flip chart
line graphs	flannelgraph
organization charts	prepared cards
flow charts	overhead projectors
pictograms	film strips
map charts	slides
	motion pictures
	opaque projectors

Any one of the types of visual aids in the left-hand column
may be presented through any of the media in the right-hand
column. Whenever possible, bring to the presentation situation any physical objects involved in your proposal. If this is
not possible, use enlarged photographs, exploded drawings,
cutaways, or models.

Be sure that all visual aids can be seen clearly by anyone
in the audience (check this out in the presentation room beforehand, when possible). Most of us groan at the opening
line, "You probably can't see this, but . . ." If they can't
see it, don't use it.

Avoid crowding visual aids with too many words or nonverbal symbols. To prevent distractions, have visual aids out
of view when not in use. When demonstrating visual aids,
look at the audience as often as possible; avoid facing the
chalkboard, chart, or screen for prolonged periods of time.

Deliver Your Presentation Professionally

A thoughtful, logical presentation can suffer from poor
delivery. Imagine hand-crafted furniture, with perfect joints

and original styling, but with scratches all over the finish. We find it difficult to appreciate quality when surface blemishes detract.

Most successful speakers avoid reading or memorizing presentations. Both of these modes of delivery tend to sound canned or unnatural, and they lack flexibility. Few people know how to write the spoken word, though playwrights, novelists, and some speechwriters have mastered the craft. When we write out a speech word for word, it tends to sound like what we produced in English Composition.

A composite mode of delivery works best for most business speakers, with primary emphasis on extemporaneous speech. An effective extempore speech requires thorough preparation of the content and organization of the presentation, with the choice of words left to the speaking occasion. In a composite speech the speaker may want to memorize a brief quotation here or there or perhaps read a complex paragraph of statistical or legal data. But the principal style of delivery is conversational, and the speaker uses a thorough outline instead of a word-by-word manuscript.

Variety means much in delivery: vary the rate of delivery, pertinently speeding up or slowing down; let natural changes occur in pitch, avoiding a limited range; and allow your volume to change, according to the meaning of what you say and feel. Avoid standing in a rigid position, and use a variety of gestures and postures, as they relevantly express what you mean.

LETTERS AND MEMOS

People have been writing letters for over two thousand years, and in all that time the basic form of the letter has changed very little. Most managers send and receive letters and memos every day. In an age of sophisticated electronic media, why do we still write letters? (1) We can produce and deliver letters relatively inexpensively. (2) Letters can be exchanged in about a week's time. (3) Each party can have a permanent, written record of the messages involved. (4) Well-written letters have a personalized quality.

What Does a Letter Say?

In a book such as this one, we will not consider the mechanics of letter writing; you can readily find that kind of information in appropriate handbooks or manuals. We will focus on tactical matters.

A letter says much more than the sum of its words or grammatical or technical aspects. Letters and memos speak about the competence, the personality, and the management style of the writer, as well as the quality and professionalism of the organization.

Have you ever received a business letter and concluded, "I'll never do business with that outfit." Have you ever read a letter and formed a silent judgment that you had little confidence in the ability or efficiency of the author? Most of us have. Whenever you send a letter, you influence relationships, attitudes, your career, and the future of your organization.

The "You" Attitude

Your primary consideration in writing a letter should focus on what the reader will think as the letter is read. You must be writing the letter for a reason—probably to inform or persuade the reader. To accomplish this, you must write the letter from the reader's perspective.

Let's use an absurd example to illustrate the point. What would you think if you received a letter which said:

My radio station is in business to make money, and right now I'm not making much. Buy some advertising time on my station as soon as possible, so I can pay my bills and begin to make a profit.

No one in the world but the author's mother (and even she might balk) would do anything about this letter except to throw it in the wastebasket or save it as an example of "how not to." Naturally we would pay much more attention to a letter which read:

You are in business to build a list of satisfied customers and to make a profit. Have you thought about how radio advertising could help you expand your business . . . ?

Basically, the "you" viewpoint asks such questions as: What does the reader need and want? What are the reader's problems? How can I help solve those problems? How does the reader see the situation? What would I do if I were in the reader's position? Why should the receiver read this letter? How can I adapt to the reader's expectations and procedures?

Tact

Occasionally, I dial long distance calls without first dialing "1." The following recording comes on, and I find myself getting irritated: "You have dialed in error." It seems to me that the telephone company could inform dialers about the correct way to dial without using the phrase "in error." No one likes to be reminded that they made an error. The telephone company could accomplish their goal, have calls completed efficiently, and make dialers happier by saying something positive such as, "To complete your call, please dial 1 before the number you are dialing. Thank you."

Tactless letters use phrases such as : "you failed to include the carbon copy of the invoice" or "we received your letter in which you claim we didn't ship the material on July 12." How much more effective it is to write: "Please send a carbon copy of the invoice so we can take care of your request" or "we're sorry you didn't receive the supplies when you needed them, though we shipped them on July 12, as we agreed to."

The refusal letter presents special problems in tact. We must often say "no" to applicants or prospective suppliers. Two important ingredients help to make a "no" letter more digestible: (1) some explanation of the reasons for the refusal; (2) any compliments or positive suggestions you may have to offer.

Dear Ms. Jones

Thank you for the excellent resume you sent with your application for employment in our Customer Relations division.

We are fully staffed in that division, and we don't expect to hire anyone for that division for at least a year; however, we will keep your application on file for several months, in case an unexpected vacancy occurs.

Recently I heard that several local banks are looking for people with your skills in Customer Relations. You might want to call the larger banks and inquire.

Sincerely yours,

Notice that the middle paragraph of the letter says "no" without using such words as "cannot use your services," "no need," "must refuse," or other negative expressions.

Emotionally-Charged Letters

Anger, resentment, hostility, and similar emotions arise in day-to-day organizational life. At one time or another most of us have thought, "I'm going to tell him off" or "I'm going to give her a piece of my mind." Maybe you should, but do you want to do it in writing on company stationery?

One helpful practice is to wait at least one day before signing or mailing one of those "I have had it!" letters. In most cases, you will probably revise the letter, set up a face-to-face situation, or perhaps forget the whole thing. One of the realities of organizational life is that we must find professionally acceptable ways to discharge such emotions as anger or hostility. Whack a golf ball, bash a punching bag, tear into some bread dough, but verbal knocks may do permanent harm. Remember that *every* letter is a public relations letter; everything you write represents you and your organization.

MANAGEMENT REPORTS

Many illustrations have been used to dramatize the knowledge explosion. For example, in some fields, the amount of information doubles between the time you matriculate in that field and the time you receive your diploma a few years later. In many specialties, you could not keep up with the new material being published each month even if you spent forty hours a week reading such material (much less read all the reams of material published in previous years).

In order to make complex decisions, managers need more and more information. Quite often, officials will delegate to various subordinates the responsibility of researching and reporting on specialized areas. Decisions are then made, based upon as much accurate data as possible.

From the dozens of management reports I have read in recent months, here are two examples. A director in an aerospace company needed many types of information in order

to complete a project. One piece of information he needed
was the necessary lead time in ordering certain types of
aluminum sheets so that the metal would be on hand when
needed. He asked one of his managers to determine the lead
time. The resulting thirty-page report specified the number
of months and days of lead time required for various manu-
facturers of the aluminum needed, and it predicted increases
in the lead time during the coming year. In another case,
an administrator in a public health agency suspected that
patients who received medical prescriptions at the agency
did not have adequate information about the nature, use,
and purpose of the medicine they were receiving. She then
designed a questionnaire and surveyed a random sample of
patients who were receiving medications at the agency. Her
study validated her suspicions, and she recommended im-
provements in the education of the patients regarding prescriptions.

Among other types of reports, the most common ones
are: periodic reports (which usually focus on performance or
production), narrative reports (which might concern accidents
or grievance situations), field surveys (what is the competition doing? what do clients want?), state-of-the-project
reports, and reports which describe problems. Many of these
types of reports (especially periodic reports) involve merely
filling in blanks on a form.

Suggested Format for Long Reports

If your organization has a preferred format for reports,
you will follow it, of course; but if such matters are left to
you, this section contains standard features for the three
main parts of a report—the prefatory elements, the main
body of the report, and the appended materials.

Prefatory Elements

The title page should contain the title of the report, the individual or group for whom the report has been written, the author(s), the organization issuing the report, and the date.

If you received a letter or authorization or delegation, assigning responsibility for the report to you, such a letter or memo may follow the title page. An effective letter of this type usually contains such items as: a clear description of the task, a clarification of the objective, an approval for any needed assistance, and a statement concerning any limitations or special problems that may arise. Since many reports are assigned orally, you may not have a letter of authorization; however, if appropriate, request one.

The letter of transmittal follows. In conveying the report to the person who authorized it, this letter includes such matters as:

1. Who assigned the report.
2. The rationale for the study.
3. Expressions of appreciation.
4. Suggestions about the use of the report.
5. Recommendations for further research.

Often letters of transmittal contain material that is usually found in prefaces or forewords. If a formal abstract or summary of the report does not appear in the report, then a digest or synopsis of the findings should be included in the letter of transmittal.

The table of contents should come right after the letter of transmittal, and probably you will type it last, since it will include pagination. Using the same headings employed in the main body of the report for sections, chapters, or any type of subject division, list the parts of the report, with page numbers. Also list any appended items.

The abstract previews the report for the reader (alas, in many cases the reader is too busy to read the report and wants only the results). In crisp language, probably in one or two paragraphs, the abstract should inform the reader of such matters as:

1. The goal and scope of the report.
2. The kind of research involved.
3. The essential findings.
4. Recommendations or conclusions.

For a report running into dozens of pages, a two- or three-page abstract might be necessary. But a tightly-written abstract need not exceed a page for most reports.

The Main Body of the Report

An introduction begins the main body of most long reports. An effective introduction orients the reader in such a way that all preliminary information is at hand for the purpose of understanding the report. This includes such information as:

1. Why the report was done.
2. The nature and extent of the study.
3. The methods of research used.
4. Needed definitions or explanations.
5. Limitations of the report.
6. Special problems in research or reporting.

Though some of these matters are outlined in the letter of transmittal or the abstract, they are explained in more detail in the introduction. The abstract tells what the reader will find; the introduction adds some hows and whys.

The actual discussion of the findings follows the introduction, and this makes up the principal part of the report. Some important criteria for the heart of the report follow:

1. *Pertinence.* Everything in the report should pertain to the assignment. If significant but irrelevant matters arise, discuss them separately.
2. *Accuracy.* Check and recheck. Use the most reliable sources and methods. Verify and reverify.
3. *Coherence.* When you read something reasonable, unified, and methodical, you don't find yourself stopping and asking, "This doesn't seem to follow" or "I don't get it" or "I can't seem to catch the thread of this."
4. *Completeness.* Without including more than you need to, all essential information must be incorporated in the report.
5. See also the suggestions on *structure* and *readability* in the preceding chapter.

The main body of the report usually ends with conclusions, recommendations, or a summary. In some cases all three might be included. If you were asked to help solve a problem, you might summarize what you found, give your conclusion about the nature, cause and effects of the problem, and then offer your recommendation(s) for solving the problem. In other cases, you might merely review the facts you discovered or present conclusions based upon your judgment and experience.

Addenda

Several types of material may be appended to the report: charts, maps, schedules, transcripts, government regulations, copies of letters, questionnaires, or various forms used in research, statistical tables, tabulations, or any kind of pertinent material which you think the reader will need for a thorough understanding of your report.

CONCLUSION

Communication theory becomes reality when we actually apply principles to specific communication activities. As you accept more and more responsibility in managing organizations, during a typical work day you will find yourself communicating most of the time. Any idea, fact, or feeling you generate will take on organizational significance only when you communicate it. I hope that the principles and practices of this chapter and of the text itself will help you communicate effectively.

SKILL DEVELOPERS

1. Secure some organizational publications (brochures, reports, bulletins), and review them for structure, format, style, accuracy, and general effectiveness.
2. With the instructor's approval, plan a class problem-solving conference. (What sort of final exam? Should there be a term paper? What should be the objectives of the course?) Evaluate the conference on the basis of appropriate passages in this chapter.
3. Plan and conduct an interview. If possible, tape the session (with the approval of the other party). Review the interview. What are the strengths? What are the areas for growth?
4. Have each member of the class give a brief oral presenta-

tion on a specific topic or proposal. Class members should give each speaker a written response covering such areas as purpose, introduction and conclusion, evidence, delivery, organization, use of visual aids, and general interest.

PANEL DISCUSSION

Rockey: Bill Perreault has a preparatory statement on using media effectively in the corporate group.

Perreault: I am dealing primarily with large organizations, because that is where I have been. I have never been in really small organizations. Your best possible medium is an eyeball-to-eyeball discussion, hopefully, with the individual or a group of people. You can sense the eye movement; you can sense the body movement; you can sense if people are comfortable or uncomfortable with what you are saying. You can see the people glance from one to another, either in agreement or disagreement, and it comes through to you. Unfortunately as your organization grows, that is limited to a very small cross section of those that you can speak to. You want to maintain that sense of continuity. That means you are addressing people on the basis of their reference point. If, in fact, people are directors and are reporting to the president's staff or to the senior management organization, then you can take them in small groups. You want to take them with some regularity. It is best to do that in the meeting environment and not send the man a memo. On the other hand, from time to time as you are spreading that message, you do have to have a method of getting the written word, because there generally is a procedure. There is something you want in writing. It is important to you that the procedure is established. Then, it seems, you revert to memorandums. We have things in our corporation called "management memos." They go only to salaried personnel. When we send that to a salaried man he knows he is getting a piece of information that is not being distributed down through the system at large. He is part of a selective management. It is on a distinctive sheet of paper; in this case yellow. He sees it in a pile, and his instinct is to go and take it out. It is like a telegram in a pile. On the other hand, we pass that point and we come to a place where we want to address

William D. Perreault

Harold Johnson

everybody in the company and tell them about a particular problem and we send out an employee bulletin. It goes to everyone. It is put into distribution boxes wherever there is a time clock around. Everyone gets it; from the president, the chairman of the board, and on down. All of these are communication lines. That communication line is rigidized. It is rather formal when it gets into that channel.

We have great belief in a level organization, in which we get key people to come together in a room one night a month in which they have a social hour and the chance to have a drink or two and a dinner. People come in to speak. We try to balance those so that about half of them are outside speakers, bringing fresh views into the environment. The other half would be part of our corporate structure. Someone from our electronics company telling what goes on in that field. Someone in our shipbuilding company. Someone associated with a major program that's currently preoccupying the company. We have a public address system. If we announce a sale of an airplane, and the sale of an airplane is multimillion dollar business, it is business that means employment for them, we'll have the president get on the public address system. He can pick up the telephone in his office. It ties him into the public address system and it will be done at the time of a work break, either a lunch break or a coffee break in the plant, and he will announce, but it has to be very short because public address systems in large dispersed places like that are not good. We have to be certain that we put some kind of a signal out, a trumpeting, which says, "Look, something is going to be said," so it gets their attention. It being a work break area, a maximum number of machines are silent and we say here is the message.

In some of our companies we use a telephone dial system, where at any time of the day, you can dial a particular telephone number and they will give you four or five items, maybe two minutes of communication on what is going on around the company. If you are really one of these people who have a desire to know what is going on, anytime you want to dial a telephone, usually twice a day they change what is on that thing, and it will tell you a little bit of what is going on around the corporation. Each of these are voice communications operated by the management we have found very effective all through the organization.

We have in every one of our divisions a company newspaper that usually comes out twice a month. We try to tell them about things which are a combination of employee interest and company interest. Each of those has a department in it in which anyone can write in any question. It is answered with complete candor from the top of the organization. If it is something sensitive, it will go up to the president's office, but it is always answered directly.

We use quite a few films and have quite a few briefings in our communication system. The films we will put on during noon hour. Through the plant and various parts of the plant we will put on films that relate to: number one, the company's activities, because we make them in pursuit of our normal business; and number two, if it is something about the capitalistic system or if it is something about an issue in which a film is available, we will play that in different areas. One plant, the one we have in New Jersey on electronics, whenever you are in the lunchroom every day, there is a carousel with 100 slides in it. Some of those slides are with messages; maybe it was the Christmas party. It just shows a continuity of slides. While you are watching and having your lunch you can see that, if you care to. It does not impose a voice track on you.

We have had as many as a dozen different publications that we have put out. We put one out, for instance, on equal opportunity to tell our employees and to tell the outside world what we do in that field. We put out something called "The Log." They are brief items, two or three line items that go to the people in the twelve different divisions. They like to know what goes on across the organization. We try to make copies of the annual report for anybody who wants it. Of course, there are the procedures—management procedures and functions and responsibilities which always go out at any given level. But I guess we are using all of the mechanisms. We play quite a lot with alternatives. We are presently discussing using some of these moving-light things like they have in Times Square or as they have on some of the bank buildings. You will get a continuous message as you come and go in prominent areas around here that tell people what we are doing. Communication is a real problem. We do not have an answer to it. We have a whole series of answers to it. We try to keep it coordinated but we find little branches coming off here and there where someone starts up a publication to serve a particular role. We like to avoid that when we can because you are sort of getting "information off the rack."

I think that a newspaper is the most effective message because people do read our newspaper. They read it for a number of reasons. In our typical four-page newspaper we have a page of classified ads. Any one in the management or anybody in this company can put an ad in, whether it is for an old baby stroller or for a new camera, to buy or sell one; an automobile. It has tremendous readership. People within a community of that size are looking for that. We are guaranteed that between our department which answers questions with considerable candor, and our classified ads, people are going to look from the front to the rear of that publication. In between there we have a lot of messages, whether it is to buy bonds or to support the United Crusade or to give them a shot in letting them know we have just received a 250 million dollar contract or that we think people should get out and vote. There is a feature in there called "The Company Is People." There is always a section that has three people in it and tells something about them and what they are doing.

Riggins: Our company is a pretty good size company, too. I certainly agree that the newspaper is most effective. We have a similar thing to what you have that we call "Intelphone." This is a method by which the employee can dial a recorder: they can ask any question, put forth any gripe they may have, or whatever, and this is handled by our employee relations department. They direct these questions to that department manager best qualified to answer promptly. Then, they are posted on the bulletin boards, throughout. That is a very effective means, too.

Perreault: Posters have been very effective in getting team spirit. On individual airplane programs, we will typically have three or four major airplane programs going here, and they do use poster programs. Number one, to instill a spirit of team in there, and also to set goals: "Fifty days before roll out, or twenty-six days before first flight, or squadron service starts in forty-five days," to give a feeling of immediacy or goal.

Rockey: If someone were making a presentation and you were listening to it, and they were seeking your approval, what are some of the things you would look for in a successful presentation?

Perreault: I have the distinct impression that I have people working around me who are eloquent; they work long hours over preparation; they have their material very well organized. They have in fact made every word count, they use the right adjectives, they put in the proper pronunciation. When they deliver it they pound home each sentence. Each phrase has a meaning. But there is no way for the recipient to pick up that much. The speaker practices for hours and polishes, and as a statement, if you read it, it is eloquent. If you examine it in detail, it is brilliant work, and the delivery is flawless. But the poor audience cannot catch ten percent of it. There is no way.

Paulson: What I hear you saying here is an issue that I am most concerned with and that is, how do you get in touch with your audience? How do you determine what people want to hear, and how do you communicate it in language which will create understanding? That is, I think, a very key element.

Rockey: Related to audience capability or audience level of interest and technical knowledge, I think they call this "sensory overload" or "information overload." Somebody gets up and throws out more than you can possibly absorb.

Perreault: I went to Georgia to talk to a group of Lockheed middle management people. We call them Lockheed Management Institutes where we take forty or fifty people from central management, and in this case Emory University has a staff handling half of the two-week period and Lockheed members of senior management come in and talk, so you get a mix of the academic and the organizational or functional activity. I was in Georgia sixteen years. I think I knew the outfit, and I felt I was going in there to talk to a group of middle management. That company has been reduced in size from 32,000 to 9,500 people. I walked in with my prepared text, which was going to be the opening gun, a launching effort, very upbeat and "go get them tiger." When I got there I found that all of those people were peers of mine of that period. They were very senior people. They are sort of retreading those people and they are presently in middle management because of tremendous shrinkage there. The man who headed flight test operations for fifteen years was one of them. The man who headed contracts for the last ten years was another one and so on through the group. So I had to throw aside what I had. My message was the wrong message totally.

Rockey: How could you have been saved from that?

Perreault: I keep saying one day I am going to write a piece called "You Owe It To The Speaker." People invite you to come and visit them in Seattle and you arrived in Seattle, and no one meets you at the airport. No one has checked out the hotel reservation. They don't make arrangements when they pick you up. They take you to a reception and there they have not bothered to make arrangements. It is a pay bar arrangement and you find yourself (1) buying your own drink, and (2) buying drinks for other people. You look around and say, "Where is the projector," and they say, "Oh, the projector. We thought *you* were bringing that." Or you ask for the projector and they say, "We have a projector, but we hope you can operate it." And it goes on through an endless cycle of these things. People don't think about the speaker. I think there is need for a text on what you owe to the speaker.

Rockey: I wish you would write that. I have spoken for many management clubs, and I'll call the program chairman beforehand and ask, "Tell me something about your club." They usually tell me how many are going to be there, what time to arrive, that they have a social hour beforehand. I really want to know what are they interested in, or what have they done lately; what does the group come there for; what do they expect.

Johnson: The middle of June I am to speak on management to a group of black health administrators. I will have about a half day. Since being requested to do it and agreeing to I have begun to find out the reality, and the reality is that I will be paying my own accommodations. The focus of the meeting is on the needs of black administrators. I have elected to speak to the point of strategy and politics and preservation of self and others. What do you really need to be an administrator? I have been unable to find out such things as the time, what size of group am I talking to, who are they. If I am talking to line-level supervisors, it is one thing, and if I am talking to executive level people, it is a totally different thing. Their needs are certainly not synonymous. As I look at this situation, the greatest need is never to go winging. Be ready to really go. But I fear I will have to wing it. That happens to me frequently.

Perreault: You can protect yourself, though in a large degree it is your own shortcoming. When I say that I am talking of *my own* experience and *my own* shortcomings. We were asked to have a speaker in an aerospace conference in Paris

on the 27th of May, staged by an important financial publication. I recommended that our company president speak, and
he reluctantly said yes, and I wrote a letter expressing our acceptance and saying what day we preferred to be on the
program and asking how long they wanted it, whether or not
there would be projection equipment and several other things
of that kind. We have now received the program back. He is
on the program. It is at the end of the first day. He is on at
5:10 in the afternoon in Paris as the *last* speaker of the day.
This is an insult. The principal people, all the press people,
will be gone; I should have made it clear to them that there
were some areas, some constraints under which he would
speak: he is going to speak within some reasonable time, and
he was not going to be the last speaker of the day, and the
question and answer period was not going to be after 6:00 p.m.
in Paris on the opening day of a major program. But that was
my responsibility and I did not carry it. I do that to myself,
which is stupid; but to do it to my president is dangerous.

Riggins: I think sometimes you can overprepare a presentation to the point that it becomes in my vernacular a "dog
and pony show." So you get up with a bunch of slides and
you go on and on and people's interest goes down. I feel that
you should go in prepared to shift gears depending on your
audience's reaction, so that if you see that you are losing
them you are prepared to shift your concept of what you
were going to do to get their attention back. Do whatever
you have to do. I think that you have to be not that set
in your preparation. You have to be more flexible.

Johnson: I think that I can identify with that in a very current and hopefully effective method in making presentations,
especially in training programs to supervisors. I will hand out
a prepared outline and disclaim it immediately. "These are
the topics we can deal with, this is how I think we could go
about it, but I am open for any way you want to go."
    It takes a great deal of charming of an audience to make
them feel free enough to volunteer. What about, "I have this

kind of problem. How do I deal with it?" To get them into the mode of consulting with the speaker is an art. It takes quite a bit of doing when you work through a few groups of unsimilar backgrounds and, rather than walk in and get started, go through quite an elaborate introduction, "Here's Harold." When you get down to where you can identify with me as a person, then what we are here for is not important. It is my job to bring us around to *that point*, not to go with my task orientation. Part of the task of administrative communication is to not be preoccupied with my time schedule but deal with what is on that person's mind; their agenda is the only one that has priority. Yours never happens.

Perreault: I have an experience with Hal's recommendation that you not be totally prepared, that you have some flexibility. I went to a productivity council meeting in London to give a talk on air cargo. I had been working on air cargo matters for some time, with a lot of money behind research on distribution cost, competitive systems, etc. Over a period of time, with a big staff, we had developed a very highly polished presentation. I would say I had given that presentation over 125 times over a period of several years, each time honing it a little bit with better illustrations and getting more to the point. And for this London meeting I put together a paper which had 76 slides; I cut it down to 30 slides for the presentation, and I spoke to the point. It was in a theater-type setting. It was excellent: a big audience, a highly polished presentation; and when I was through I had a good reaction—no questions: that is, no *organized* questions. But when I came down off the stage one man came to me and said, "That was one of the best presentations I ever heard. The illustrations were beautiful and the subject matter was precise for the aim of this particular conference, and your delivery was eloquent. But as a friend, I have to tell you one thing. If you want to have any credibility, you have got to introduce some amateurism into this effort. Absolutely nobody in England will believe a presentation which is made in the form you have made this one."

Rockey: Too slick?

Perreault: Yes, too slick. It was a big polished road show, and they do not want that. A lot of people do not want it. If you are a dedicated meeting-goer, and you are sick of people rambling, you may want that. But that is not what this audience wanted. People like to relate.

Riggins: It is difficult to relate to an audience standing at a podium, if you are frozen to that podium. If you can—this is not always the case—you cannot do it sometimes—but if you can wander around a little bit during your presentation, I think your body speaks as well as your mouth. You can come across, you can get the people to think, "Okay, he is one of us—just like us—and he is talking to us," you can express yourself in a more meaningful way if you have a little freedom of movement.

Paulson: Last year I was asked to speak for National Women's Recognition Week on the topic of "The Changing Role of Women in the Business World." I went prepared with a presentation and a speech, and there were two other panel members who were going to follow me. The two panel members showed up and they were just going to wing it. I was really ready to go. I started my presentation on where I felt women had come from, what their role in business was, what business was looking for in women managers. I had a room full, sixty-five women ranging from eighteen through somewhere in the neighborhood of sixty years old. I said, "Feel free to interrupt me at any point if you want to discuss what I am talking about." I got halfway through and one gal said, "How did you get where you got?"

For a moment, I must confess, I was absolutely stunned. I thought, "Gee, what do you mean?" "Go ahead, tell me about your career progression." I ended up going down off the stage, sitting dead center in the middle of them, and discussing the situation, which was a very productive opportunity for me and very productive for the people that were attending, but totally aside from what I felt I was to be presenting.

Rockey: What are some key things you have found helpful in dictating correspondence; letters, memos, minutes, reports; are there any techniques that help you?

Riggins: I think, for the person that is first starting, to organize what you want to say. Jot down a little note on each topic, just a single-line type thing, on each subject or the organizational structure you want to accomplish. That makes your lead-in and you can follow that. I think it is a direct aid to the person that is not accustomed to dictating a lot.

Perreault: There are a couple of issues that strike me. One of them is that, in my opinion, 99 out of 100 people do not know how to dictate. Mostly, they do not know how to dictate because they were not born with the ability to dictate and they are never willing to develop the art. They do not want to show their ignorance. They do not want to expose themselves. They do not want to have to go back and do things over. So they build up various forms of crutches. If, in fact, they were to spend a year and go through some of those embarrassments and develop the flow, then dictation would be the only way. So it is very prevalent. In that regard, in developing the flow, we use blackboards all through the place. People tend to go to the board when they have meetings, and when you are through you generally have something you can go back to and dictate from. The blackboard just happens to be a very useful tool for that type of thing. When you sit down to dictate the combined ideas are up there on the board.

Paulson: I wholeheartedly agree with Bill about developing your skills. It frees you from so many things, and it is an effective utilization of your time and creates a whole lot more job satisfaction for the people who support you. They are really very willing to go through that process because then, once they have "the tapes," they can schedule their own time and priority.

Rockey: It is sort of cutting the umbilical cord to get away from, "Enclosed, herewith, please find per your request."

But, "What am I going to say if I do not say that?" It is challenging and awkward at first to develop a clear, crisp style. But it is well worth the investment.